First Logic

John Humphrey
Minnesota State University

KENDALL/HUNT PUBLISHING COMPANY
4050 Westmark Drive   Dubuque, Iowa 52002

Cover image © Artville

Contents

Preface

This book is intended to introduce students to the ancient art and science of logic and, more generally, the art and science of thinking. For me, logic comprises the methods and principles used in distinguishing correct reasoning from incorrect reasoning. In this sense it is a normative discipline. Logic is also an activity, one that includes the activity of criticizing reasoning, one's own, as well as that of others. More specifically, I believe that the best way to teach logic is to treat it as a skill, like reading, writing, adding, subtracting, and yes, playing golf and tennis. We acquire and master these skills by using them, by practicing them, by trying to improve them. Occasionally, we find that a bit of information about an activity can help improve our performance of the activity but for the most part, the best way to acquire a skill is not by reading about it but by actually doing it. That is why this text tries to offer a larger ratio of exercises to exposition than other texts I have encountered over the years.

In some sense, my philosophy of teaching logic is that once a student masters the skill, s/he can be left on his/her own to confront the world and make sense of it as s/he logically sees fit. Over the years, I have discovered that students come to college or university with a rather diverse set of logical skills and abilities. Simply put, some students need very little instruction in logic while others need a good deal more instruction, not to mention encouragement, support, coaxing, prodding, and practice most of all.

The aim of this book is to allow students to improve their logical skills and reasoning abilities. This is not to say that the line between correct and incorrect reasoning is a hard and fast one, nor that there is universal agreement in all cases as to where the line between the two gets drawn. However, logic, since it is only slightly less ancient a subject than reasoning itself, admits of much that is stable and secure. This text will focus, in large part, on those stable and secure areas while occasionally offering a directional pointer or two at less stable matters.

I would like to express my thanks to all of my teachers from whom I learned to reason and think. Your efforts seem not to have been in vain. And, of course, I want to give thanks to my wife, Judith for love, comfort, understanding and discourse. She is the *sine qua non* of my life and work. My children, David and Samantha must also be mentioned here because the life of the material in this book coincides very nearly with their own lives. As they grew, so did I. And as I grew so too did this book. Finally, whatever blunders or infelicities are awaiting discovery in the actual using of the text, are mine alone. At this point, I can only apologize for them in advance and promise to repair them in the next incarnation of this book.

Introduction

'I know what you're thinking about,' said Tweedledum: 'but it isn't so, nohow.'
'Contrariwise,' continued Tweedledee, 'if it was so, it might be; and if it were so, it would be: but as it isn't, it ain't. That's logic.   Lewis Carroll

If pressed to supplement Tweedledee's ostensive definition of logic with a discursive definition of the same subject, I would say that logic is the systematic study of the logical truths. Pressed further, I would say that a sentence is logically true if all sentences with its grammatical structure are true.   W. V. Quine, famous American logician

Logic is an ancient discipline whose official origins go back to Aristotle's *Organon* in the middle of the 4th century B.C. Unofficially, of course, its origins are to be found in the first thinking by a human being, whoever he or she may have been. In order to think, in any important sense of the word, one needs a language. And so it is likely that the first logician was also the first language-user, since thinking and language are inextricably linked and both involve a bit of logic. So intimate is the connection between thought and language that anyone reading this page has already mastered many of the most important parts of the thinking, and thus logic, game. In learning language one learns logic. Not in its entirety, of course, but enough of it to make learning the elements of logic a relatively painless process.

To illustrate this, consider a simple example. Suppose I tell you: George Bush is in Texas playing golf. You could respond to this claim in many different ways. You might ask: How is he playing? Or you might joke: I hope he has a better round than he had yesterday. Or you could lament: Why must he play so much golf? You could moralize: He ought not play so much golf when there are troops in the Middle East. You could express a wish: I hope he gets a hole in one today. You could perform an action: I hereby dub W the nation's luckiest person. Or you could respond with a claim like: Bush isn't in Washington doing the nation's business. I take it that many would agree that this last claim is true *given the fact that* Bush is currently playing golf in Texas. It's the last of these responses that involves the use of logic most directly.

When someone claims, as in the last example above, that the truth of one statement permits us to affirm another statement, s/he is making an inference and thus performing the most basic and important of logical tasks. Although we take the ability to do this more or less for granted in many cases, and in many cases do it quite well without thinking very much about it, it's helpful to acquaint oneself with the basic rules of the logic game and to consciously examine and understand them. Doing so will not only help one become a better and more informed thinker but it will also enable one to better assess the reasoning of others. And that is a valuable skill.

Of course, knowing how various statements and sentences hang, or do not hang, together, is all very well and good but in order for us to know whether a statement inferred from another statement is in fact true, won't we need to know whether the statement we infer from is true? Of course, the answer to this question is YES. And, truth be told, it's also the case that logic is not really in the business of determining whether individual statements are true or false. Or, as I like to say, one dirty little secret about logic is that logic alone will not, except in a few fringe cases, help us to determine whether some particular statement is true or false.

Nonetheless, all of us know that if it is true that Bush is in Texas golfing then it is true that he isn't in Washington working. We know this because we understand the two sentences and understand at least one important logical relation between them. Roughly speaking, we know the second sentence is true if the first sentence is true. Of course, being able to determine when one or more sentences being true permits us to claim that another sentence is true, is not always as easy as the example about George Bush. Still, such is the basic idea even though its application gets a bit more complex in particular cases.

Logic is, as suggested above, the art of knowing when it is legitimate (or wise or justified or rational, etc.) to infer one claim from other claims.

One complicating factor however is that you can make many inferences from the claim that Bush is playing golf in Texas. You could infer: Bush can't be in Florida sunning, or you could infer: Bush is not in Minnesota walleye fishing, or: Bush is not in California skateboarding, or: Bush is not in New Mexico weaving, etc. Obviously many different inferences, indeed, many that we have no desire to make, can be had at the price of one single claim about the President's current golf game. And though, practically speaking, we never have any need to generate all possible inferences from our claims, any inferences we care to draw can be assessed for legitimacy by the techniques set out in this book.

The remarks above suggest, ever so slightly, that the general nature of logic is quite similar to the general nature of arithmetic and mathematics. When you learn to do addition and subtraction you learn a general technique that can be applied to almost anything at all. Counting chickens, counting money, counting golf strokes, counting students, etc., all involve the same technique of addition and you have no trouble applying this technique to new situations and objects. Similarly, once you have mastered the skill of drawing inferences, you will have no trouble applying this skill in new situations, to new subjects and new sentences.

As already suggested, perhaps the most important part of the game of logic is learning how to distinguish good inferences from bad ones and strong ones from weak ones. For example, from the statement that George Bush is currently playing golf in Texas someone might claim to know: He has his trusty putter with him.

Now what, if anything, is the difference between this claim and our previous inference: Bush isn't in Washington working? The obvious answer is that the two claims differ with respect to *certainty*. We want to say that it absolutely, positively has to be true that Bush isn't in Washington if he is in Texas, whereas it is possible that he is currently playing golf in Texas but without his trusty putter. For example, Bush's dog may have taken the trusty putter from Bush's bag and buried it in the backyard and Bush didn't notice it until he got to the first hole and rather than hold up the group, he decided he would use his father's putter instead. Thus anyone who claims to know that since Bush is playing golf in Texas he must have his trusty putter, could be reminded of the possibility that Bush's playful dog (or a competitor!) has removed the putter from Bush's bag and thereby challenge the truth of the claim: Bush has got his trusty putter with him. And the fact that this challenge can be made is enough to show that the inference: Bush has his trusty putter with him, differs from the inference: Bush isn't in Washington working. That, as Lewis Carroll might say, is logic.

A more formal way of looking at this is to say that the claim:

(1) If George Bush is in the middle of his daily golf game in Texas then he has his trusty putter with him,

is possibly false, whereas:

(2) If George Bush is in the middle of his daily golf game in Texas then he isn't in Washington working, is obviously true.

Among other things, mastering the art of logic involves mastering the art of distinguishing if-then statements one from another on the basis of their possible truth and falsity.

So far we have mentioned only simple inferences, that is, those that involve drawing a consequence from a single statement. But, of course, real life is more complicated than that. Most often, inferences are drawn from at least two different claims, and when they are we say that an **argument** has been given. More formally, I'll say that an argument consists of at least three claims. In any argument, there will always be one and only one claim that is being argued for and this is called the **conclusion**. The claims that are given as support for the conclusion are called **premises**. Some logicians, myself included on occasion, regard inferences drawn from a single claim to be arguments as well. There is nothing wrong with this use of 'argument' but most real life arguments do involve more than a single premise. To mark this fact, I prefer to speak of a claim inferred from a single claim as an immediate inference rather than an argument. Another reason for distinguishing immediate inferences from arguments is that we will want to speak of the form of arguments and the notion of form does not apply very easily

3

to immediate inferences. Still, I am not particularly fussy about the distinction (see chapter 5) and so allow myself and others to speak of one premise arguments when they find it convenient to do so.

A Semi-Technical Distinction – Contingent and Necessary

Philosophers and logicians distinguish between at least two kinds of sentences and getting comfortable with this distinction goes a long way toward getting comfortable with logic. But we need to work up to this distinction by reminding ourselves of an important fact. We saw above that not all sentences of the English language are used to make true-false claims. In fact, English sentences can be compared usefully to the tools in a toolbox. All of the tools in a toolbox have a somewhat unique function or use and the same goes for the expressions of language that we use every day. Logicians concentrate on the expressions of language that are used to make true-false claims as opposed to statements used to ask a question, issue a command, express a wish, tell a joke, perform a function, stroke others, etc. For example, 'Pigs are filthy' is a true-false claim whereas 'Are pigs filthy?' and 'Clean those pigs!' and 'Why must pigs be so filthy?' are not. Getting clear on the distinctions between the various uses to which sentences can be put is the concern of a discipline called *pragmatics* and philosophy of language generally, and so will not be pursued further in this book. From this moment on we will simply agree to confine ourselves to the use of true-false claims. Such sentences are also called *declarative sentences*, or *fact-stating sentences*, as well. (More on these sentences in chapter 4 below).

We are now in a position to make the distinction mentioned above. Among the sentences used to make true-false claims, some are said to be *contingent* statements while others are said to be *necessary* statements. One way of making this distinction is to say that contingent statements are those that, if true, one can imagine them to be false, and if false, can imagine them to be true. In contrast, necessary statements, if true, cannot be imagined to be false and if false, cannot be imagined to be true. More succinctly, contingent statements are true-false claims that can be imagined to be otherwise whereas necessary statements cannot be imagined to be otherwise.

One problem with this way of marking the distinction between contingent statements and necessary statements is that it appeals to imagination and it may very well be that you and I have different ideas about what can and what cannot be imagined. Indeed, some philosophers, to use the old saying, "have a cow", whenever someone tries to make the distinction between necessary and contingent statements by appeal to imagination. However, academics have a tendency to state things in quite hysterical ways and frankly, such hysterical academics need not interest us overmuch. I think that our imaginations are very much linked to our language and I think our common language is a source of vast agreement among

4

language-users as to what can and what cannot be imagined. Consequently, we can lean on language understanding/imagination to establish widespread agreement as to which statements are contingent and which are necessary. Let's look at some examples.

The following are all *contingent* statements:

> Some dogs have fleas.
> It's raining outside.
> Groucho Marx is funny.
> Venus is the morning star.

Of course, the list could be extended indefinitely. Whatever the actual truth-value of these statements, it's clear that we could imagine that actual truth-value being otherwise than it is. For example, we can imagine a world completely devoid of fleas, a sunny day, and an unfunny Groucho Marx (difficult, I know) in which case the first three sentences would all be false. And we could imagine that the astronomical object dubbed the morning star on one fine day was in fact not Venus.

Now contrast those sentences with the following necessary statements:

> If some dogs have fleas then some dogs have fleas.
> Either it's raining outside or it's not.
> All funny people are funny.
> Venus is the morning star and Venus is not the morning star.

It is obvious that each of these statements is either necessarily true or necessarily false. They can't be otherwise than they are, at least not while also making any sense. Of course, one significant feature of these necessary statements is that they do not provide us with much information about the way things are. For example, if I ask someone about the weather and s/he replies: Either it's raining outside or it's not, I would not really have been told anything about the weather that I didn't already know, or that I couldn't have known without even looking. Still, as useless as necessary statements are for passing along information they are very important for determining the legitimacy of deductions and thereby the validity of deductive arguments.

The importance of necessary statements for determining the validity of deductions and deductive arguments is due to the rather startling fact that all and only valid deductive arguments correspond to a necessarily true *if-then* sentence. We have already had an example of a necessarily true *if-then* sentence in (2) above (from page 3). And (1) above (from page 3) is an example of a contingent *if-then* sentence. Using our fussy terminology above we could say that (2) would yield a valid *immediate inference* whereas (1) would not.

Distinguishing contingent statements from necessary statements is not always a straightforward and uncontroversial affair. In some cases, people disagree. Be this as it may, there are plenty of cases that are not controversial and about which there is wide agreement. This allows us to regard the distinction as both viable and useful and leave the controversial cases for another time. In order to get comfortable with this distinction, I have provided a few exercises below.

Exercises

I. Which of the following sentences are contingent and which are necessary? If you detect an ambiguity, say what it is and how it affects your answer.

1. St. Louis, Missouri is in Missouri.
2. There are 3,665 cities in the state of Missouri.
3. Dan Quayle is the vice-president of the United States.
4. There is no life on Earth.
5. John Huston directed *Beat the Devil* and *The African Queen*.
6. The director of *Beat the Devil* is John Huston.
7. Some numbers are transcendental.
8. If no freshpersons are upperclasspersons then no upperclasspersons are freshpersons.
9. If no singers are pacifists then no pacifists are singers.
10. If no Jews are Christians then no Christians are Jews.
11. All's well that ends well.
12. When everything is said and done, there's nothing left to say or do.

II. Mark each of the less than straightforward claims below as either contingent or necessary.

1. This statement is not true.
2. No evil can befall the good man.
3. No one does evil knowingly.
4. No one can see the world except through his or her own spectacles.
5. Everything that exists is material.
6. If an irresistible force meets an immovable object then nothing will happen.
7. If God is all-powerful then he can create a rock so heavy that he can not lift it.
8. If there are at least 8 people in the room then at least two of them were born on the same day of the week.
9. If train A leaves from Boston for New York at noon (and travels at 90 miles per hour) while train B leaves from New York for Boston an hour later (traveling at 65 mph) then train B will be closer to Boston when they meet.
10. According to proper English usage, it is more correct to say the yolk *is* white than to say the yolk *are* white.
11. When the going gets tough, the tough get going.
12. Sticks and stones can break your bones but words can never harm you.

III. Immediate Inferences. For each of the following, decide whether (b) can be legitimately deduced from (a).

1. (a) Only truthful persons are admitted to heaven.
   (b) Every truthful person is admitted to heaven.
2. (a) All who like angling love virtue.
   (b) All who don't like virtue don't like angling.
3. (a) All who are admitted have a ticket.
   (b) All who don't have a ticket are not admitted.
4. (a) Politicians are as dishonest as they are greedy.
   (b) Politicians are dishonest and greedy.
5. (a) Good athletes are as strong as they are agile.
   (b) Good athletes are strong and agile.
6. (a) If you drink poison you'll die.
   (b) If you don't drink poison you won't die.
7. (a) If you have sex you'll get pregnant
   (b) If you don't have sex you won't get pregnant.
8. (a) If Jack sinks this putt then he wins the tournament.
   (b) If Jack doesn't sink this putt then he loses the tournament.
9. (a) The sauna is available to anyone who is a registered guest or
       who pays a $10 fee.
   (b) The sauna is available to anyone who is both a registered guest
       and who pays a $10 fee.
10. (a) Anyone who gets an A on both of the first two tests or who gets
        an A on the final will get an A for the course.
    (b) Anyone who gets an A on both of the first two tests as well as an A
        on the final will not get an A for the course.
11. (a) Only men are allowed in combat.
    (b) Men are only allowed in combat.
12. (a) Everything that happens has a meaning.
    (b) There is a meaning to everything that happens.
13. (a) Every meal we serve is backed by our guarantee.
    (b) Our guarantee backs every meal we serve.
14. (a) Everybody loves somebody.
    (b) Somebody is loved by everybody.
15. (a) Some of her work is top-notch.
    (b) Some of her work is not top-notch.
16. (a) Some, but not all, of the apples are ripe.
    (b) Some of the apples are not ripe.
17. (a) Jack's golf score today was sub-par.
    (b) Jack's golf score was under par today.
18. (a) The biggest Viking fans come from Mankato.
    (b) Mankato is where the biggest Viking fans come from.

Chapter 1: Puzzles and Problems for Fun

... it is a wholesome plan, in thinking about logic, to stock the mind with as many puzzles as possible, since these serve much the same purpose as is served by experiments in physical science.
Bertrand Russell from "On Denoting"

The following puzzles require a variety of reasoning skills to solve them. They are basically mental calisthenics. More important than your answers are the arguments that you could give to others to convince them that your answers are correct. Enjoy.

1. Whoever shredded the crop report had corporate clearance, was in the meeting room on Friday, had knowledge of hedge funds, and had access to the bizhub. Only those who know stocks have knowledge of hedge funds. All who have access to the bizhub have corporate clearance. No one but Steph, Hal, Mark and Gabby was in the meeting room on Friday. Steph does not have access to the bizhub unless Mark has knowledge of hedge funds. Hal has access to the bizhub but Gabby lacks corporate clearance. Mark knows nothing about stocks. Who shredded the crop report?

2. The average temperature in Kurdjistan on New Year's Day (expressed to the nearest degree) has been different for each of the last five years. The product of these temperatures is 12. What are the five temperatures?

3. Mrs. Smith, her brother, her son, and her daughter all work for the post office. Of these four, the one who draws the highest salary is of the opposite sex to the twin of the one whose salary is lowest. The one who is highest paid and the one who is lowest paid are the same age. Who is the highest paid, and who is the lowest paid?

4. Ten ping pong balls each had a number from 1 to 10 and were put into a container. Al, Bob, Cliff, Darlene and Everett, in that order, drew out and kept two balls each. The sum total of the two numbers on their balls in each case was as follows: Al, 16; Bob, 11; Cliff, 4; Darlene, 17; and Everett, 7. Can you determine the numbers on each person's ping pong balls? If so, what are they?

5. Of three prisoners in a jail, one had two working eyes, a second man had only one working eye, while the third prisoner was completely blind. Another important fact is that although none of the prisoners was a likely candidate for MENSA, each man was more than able to do a bit of logical reasoning. The jailer brought the men together one day to give them a chance to be set free. He told the prisoners that from five hats, three white hats and two red hats, he would select three hats and put one on each prisoner's head. The jailer told them that any of

them who could guess the color of his particular hat from seeing only the hats of his fellow prisoners, would be set free. So the jailer put the hats on each prisoner's head and first asked the man with normal vision if he knew the color of his hat. Since the penalty for a wrong answer was execution, the first man did not want to simply guess and after seeing the hats on his fellow prisoners, he admitted that he did not know the color of his hat. The second prisoner was then asked the same question and he too said that he did not know the color of his hat. The jailer was about to leave, thinking that the blind man was not likely to hazard a guess without seeing the hats on the other prisoners. But the blind prisoner insisted that he knew the color of his hat. Is this possible and, if so, what color hat does the blind man have? Finally, if he can know, can you explain how he knows?

6. Each speaker says the following and nothing more: Andrew says that Bill is lying; Bill says that Carol is lying; Carol says that both Andrew and Bill are lying. Which of these people, if any, is telling the truth and how do you know this?

7. Troy wants to marry a girl who is intelligent, beautiful and rich. His opportunities are limited to four girls, at least one of which has all three traits mentioned above: Amber, Bebe, Candy and Daphne. Of them, three are intelligent, two are rich, and only one is beautiful, though each has at least one of these traits. Amber and Bebe are alike in net worth. Bebe and Candy are equal in intelligence while Candy and Daphne differ in intelligence. Who should Troy marry?

8. The owner of Bad Bill's Barbeque is going to give $56 to 10 loyal customers at his restaurant. Each customer is either a man or a woman. The owner will give each female customer $6, while each male customer is to get $5. How many men and how many women are there among the 10 customers?

9. An antique collector bought a desk for $6, sold it for $7, bought it back for $8, and sold it again for $10. How much profit did the collector make on these transactions?

10. A certain convention numbered 50 lawyers. Each lawyer was either crooked or honest. We are given the following two facts:
(1) At least one of the lawyers was honest.
(2) Given any two of the lawyers, at least one of the two was crooked.
How many of the lawyers were honest and how many were crooked?

11. In a certain group, each member was either a theist or an atheist. One day one of the atheists decided to become a theist, and after this happened, there were an equal number of theists as atheists. A few weeks later, the new theist decided to become an atheist again, and so things were back to normal. Then another theist

decided to become an atheist, at which point there were twice as many atheists as theists. What was the original makeup of the group?

12. Another Hat Problem: There are seven hats: two orange, two blue and three green hats. A, B and C are given hats a la problem #5. A is asked: Do you know one color that you definitely do not have? He replied, NO. B was asked the same question and also answered, NO. C says that he now knows the color of his hat. Can he know this? If so, what is the color of C's hat?

13. Three students and three professors have to cross a river. The boat they have is big enough for only two people (I know, get a bigger boat). The students generally behave themselves except that they are hungry and whenever there are more students than professors on one side of the river then the students will eat the professors. (This includes the cases when a student is already on the shore and a student and professor arrive in a boat on the same shore.)

What is the most economical plan for crossing the river so that no professor gets eaten?

14. You come upon A, B, and C. A says: Exactly two of us are knights. B says: No, that's not right, only one of us is a knight. C says: B is telling the truth. What are A, B, and C?

15. Is the following situation possible, by your lights?

A woman claims to have two and only two coins in her pocket, both of which are U.S. coins. The combined worth of the coins is 30 cents and one of them is not a nickel.

16. What are the chances that from a random selection of eight people in the class that I will find at least two people who are born on the same day of the week?

Chapter 2: Logic and Language – What Are We Talking About?

Philosophy attempts, not to discover new truths about the world, but to gain a clear view of what we already know and believe about it. That depends upon attaining a more explicit grasp of the structure of our thoughts; and that in turn on discovering how to give a systematic account of the working of language, the medium in which we express our thoughts.   Michael Dummett

Logic: The art of thinking and reasoning in strict accordance with the limitations and incapacities of the human misunderstanding.   Ambrose Bierce in *The Devil's Dictionary*

Logic, as should be clear from the introduction, is intimately related to language. As I often say, to know a language is to know a great deal of logic and to know how to think. The first part of this book covers material that every competent language user is acquainted with, however dimly. The only difficulty, and I use the term loosely, that students encounter in this part of logic lies in mastering the terminology and formalizations that philosophers and logicians use to describe and categorize the key elements of language. Even so, the basic notions of this part of the course are more unfamiliar than they are difficult.

Although logic is commonly and rightly thought to be concerned with how the truth of one sentence bears on the truth of another, a bit of reflection shows that in order to know how sentences relate one to another requires knowing something about sentences themselves. Most sentences of natural language involve two key components, a subject, or something the sentence is about, and a predicate, or something that is ascribed to, or said of, the subject.

As far as subjects go, one important distinction in logic, and language, is that between general terms and singular terms. General terms can be rather fussily defined as any term that purports to apply to, or be true of, more than one thing or object. On the other hand, singular terms can be defined as any term that purports to apply to, or be true of, exactly one thing or object. This distinction is simple but vital to language and thought, and so logic as well.

General Terms
General term: any term that purports to be true of more than one thing or object.

Examples of general terms include 'dog', 'people', 'baseball bat', 'shirt', 'color', 'apple pie', 'justice', 'compact disc', etc. Each of these terms purport to be true of more than one thing or object. As these examples make clear, general terms are parts of our language that help us organize the buzzing, blooming world of particular sights, sounds and objects that we encounter every day. They do this by serving as labels for useful collections of objects among which we find some sort of similarity or resemblance. General terms help us organize the vast world of individuals and particulars by bringing together things that are similar in various ways, ways that we deem to be significant for one reason or another.

The general terms for particular kinds of animals that we all learn early in life, for example, 'dog', enshrines the fact that we find a resemblance between particular dogs that is worth noting in language. Ditto for particular cats and the general term 'cat', particular horses and the general term 'horse', etc. Of course, dogs, cats and horses also resemble each other in ways that are worth remarking on, which yields the general term, 'animal', and so on, as we'll see in more detail below.

Singular Terms and Referents

Singular term: Any term that purports to be true of exactly one thing.

Examples of singular terms include 'Plato', 'Martin Luther', 'Albert Einstein', as well as, 'the current president of the United States', 'that gentleman on the tee box', and 'the author of *Methods of Logic*'. The first three examples are proper names, while the latter three are examples of definite descriptions. Although philosophers have said much about the differences between proper names and definite descriptions, for our purposes the alleged differences between them will be unimportant. Still, it is worth appreciating that whereas proper names seem to be mere labels, that is, we use them simply to refer to some particular thing or other (Plato, by any other name, would be as philosophical), definite descriptions have some content or meaning about them and in order to understand what it is they apply to, requires understanding that content. The bottom line however is that both sorts of expressions are singular terms, that is, both purport to apply to, or be true of, exactly one thing on any particular occasion.

Proper names seem not to have intension or meaning. Their job seems to be simply that of identifying some particular object. Definite descriptions, on the other hand, seem to have a meaning and what they refer to is a function of that meaning. As such, 'the teacher of Aristotle' and 'the author of the *Republic*' clearly differ in meaning but pick out the same object, viz., Plato.
As for 'Plato', whatever meaning it might have in the Greek (allegedly, the word connotes being broad, either in shoulders or head; some have suggested it can be used to mean "fathead") is not the point. 'Plato' is simply a label for a particular person on any particular occasion of its use. If one is interested in what philosophers have said about the difference between names and descriptions a good place to look is Saul Kripke's *Naming and Necessity*.

The individual things or objects that a general term is true of are called referents of the general term. For example, some of the referents of 'dog' include Fido, Rover, Spot, Rin-Tin-Tin, Lassie, etc. So referents of the general term 'dog' are individual dogs that we can pet, play with, feed, clean up after, etc. The same cannot be said of general terms themselves. This is because, as noted above, general terms are our creation, our terms for a group of individual that we have deemed worthy of being lumped together, for one reason or another. Notice too, and this is important, that in each of the above examples, the referents were identified via a singular term. That is no accident: Referents of concepts are always identified via singular terms.

Singular terms then can play two roles in language. First, they can be subject terms in sentences, (thus, 'Plato is a philosopher of antiquity') and second, we can use them to specify particular referents of our general terms (thus, 'Pepper' is a referent of the general term, 'cat').

It is worth noting that between any two particular objects, for example, Socrates and the current president of the United States, one can readily find some resemblance or other between them. In fact, one can usually find a large number of similarities or resemblances between particular objects. For example, Socrates and George Bush are both human beings, both are mortal, both are male, both are bipedal, both are born of woman, etc., etc., as far as the imagination cares to continue. These various resemblances are encapsulated in our general terms, 'human being', 'mortal', 'male', 'bipedal', 'born of woman', etc. Of course, these terms themselves are amalgams of various general terms. For example, the general term, 'human being', is most readily and easily explained by two other general terms, namely, 'rational' and 'animal'. And each of these terms in turn are an amalgam of still more general terms, including 'living thing', 'organism', 'possessed of sense organs', etc.

Different general terms, for example, 'human' and 'bus', mark the different ways that we humans regard particular things as resembling each other. If we happen to be in a very generalizing mood, we can lump everything together via the general term, 'existent', or 'presently a part of the universe'. When we want to make finer distinctions, we might move from 'animal' to 'fish' to 'freshwater fish' to 'game fish' to 'perch', and finally to Minnesota's state fish, 'walleye'.

As for singular terms, their role is to enable us to identify individuals. Of course, once general terms and singular terms are in place, we are then able to talk about the things that are identified by each sort of term. That is, general terms and singular terms serve as subjects in our statements about the world. And it is our statements about the world that enable us to say things that are true or false. From there, we are able to string statements about the world together into arguments. But before we get ahead of ourselves, we need to examine the machinery related to the general terms of language in a bit more detail.

Of course, if we like, we can certainly apply our general term/referent talk to itself. We already have the general term, 'general term', and its referents include 'dog', 'cat', 'animal', 'vegetable', 'mineral', etc. Notice that it is not dogs that are said to be referents of 'general term'. That would be an obvious, but nonetheless commonly committed, mistake, because dogs are animals, not terms. Rather, the referents of 'general term' are terms, namely, 'dog', 'cat', 'fish', etc. (See chapter 3 on definitions for how the single quote marks work).

Also, the matter of general terms that are true of nothing, as well as that of singular terms that name nothing, has not been ignored by logicians or philosophers. On the contrary, it's probably fair to say that it has received more attention than it deserves, starting with the Greek philosopher Parmenides, who mused, in strange but influential ways, about whether thought, or talk, of nothing made any sense. He claimed it did not but many disagreed. For anyone interested in this potentially consuming topic, a good start would be Bertrand Russell's "On Denoting", followed by P.F. Strawson's "On Referring", followed by W.V. Quine's essay, "On What There Is".

Extension and Intension

In the case of general terms, logicians have long distinguished between a term's *extension* and its *intension*. Roughly speaking, the extension of a general term concerns the things or objects the general term applies to, or is true of. Thus, the extension of the general term 'dog' is simply the set of all dogs (real or imagined, if you like, past, present and to come, if you like), the extension of the general term 'professor' is simply the set of all professors, and so on.

In contrast, the intension of a general term is the criteria (or rule) that we use to determine what objects or things the general term applies to or is true of. More simply, a term's intension is the criteria we use to determine which things belong in the extension of the general term. Whether you bother to appreciate it or not, when you apply some general term to things of your experience and refuse to apply it to other things of your experience, you appeal to some criteria or other that warrants applying, or not applying, the term in question. Of course, this way of putting things makes the whole process sound a bit more complex than it is for we seasoned speakers. Another way of understanding the intension of a general term, and a much more familiar way of regarding it, is to see it as pretty much the same thing as the meaning of the general term.

Although questions about what words mean and how they do so are quite interesting and worth pursuing, it's safe to say that philosophers have written much more about meaning than deserves to be read. For our purposes, one point worth keeping in mind is that two general terms may be true of the same things (that is, have identical extension) but yet have different criteria for membership in the extension (that is, differ in intension). In short, general terms can have the same extension but different intension.

W.V. Quine, the famous American logician, liked to illustrate this fact by speaking of 'cordates', or creatures with a heart, and 'renates', or creatures with kidneys. In our world, it turns out that 'cordate' and 'renate' have the same extension, that is, are true of the same creatures. But we can appreciate that the criteria used to distinguish cordates from things that are not cordates (namely, non-creatures and creatures without hearts) differs from the criteria used to distinguish renates from non-renates. So we see that identical extension does not guarantee identical intension. Of course, identical intension does guarantee identical extension. For this reason, some recommend taking the intension of a general term to be its defining characteristic, that is, take it as the basis for deciding when two general terms are identical or not.

On the other hand, the difficulty of coming up with intensions for terms that satisfy all comers, leads some to favor an extensional approach to language. Although it is easy enough in a great number of cases to provide an adequate account of the intension of our terms, it is also quite difficult if not impossible to do so, in other cases. Ever since Socrates went around asking his fellow Athenians to define terms like 'temperance', 'courage', 'piety', 'friendship', 'virtue', 'justice', etc., philosophers have been painfully aware that articulating the intension of various terms is tricky business. If you suppose otherwise, do yourself a favor and read some of Plato's dialogues, including "Meno", "Protagoras", "Euthyphro", or book I of Plato's classic, *Republic*.

In some contexts, for example, mathematical contexts especially, it is both possible and quite useful to identify general terms, or sets of things, by their extensions only. That is, to regard general terms which have the same extensions to be identical. This is part of taking an extensional view of language, which amounts to ignoring the properties one uses in bringing the class of objects together. It is controversial whether an extensional language is sufficient for doing justice to our knowledge of the world. If one is interested in the controversy, a good read is W.V. Quine's widely anthologized paper, "Two Dogmas of Empiricism".

One more case of intension. As noted above, proper names contrast with general terms in not having intension or meaning. Rather, the primary job of a proper name is to allow us to identify some particular object. Definite descriptions are different, however. 'The teacher of Aristotle' and 'the author of the *Republic*' clearly differ in meaning but pick out the same object, Plato. This difference gives rise to another dispute about extensional and intensional uses of terms. When different singular terms that pick out the same object can be substituted for each other in sentences without affecting the truth-value of the sentence, the context for the singular terms is said to be extensional. A typical case of an extensional context is identity statements. Thus, in the sentence, 'Plato is the author of the *Republic*', any term that refers to Plato can be substituted for 'the author of the *Republic*', preserving the truth. But the same cannot be said for the sentence, 'Tom believes that Plato is the author of the *Republic*'. We cannot be sure that any term that refers to Plato can be substituted for 'the author of the *Republic*' in this sentence while preserving the truth. (We will examine why in chapter 4). As such, the latter sentence is said to have its singular terms in an intensional context. If one is interested in questions about names, descriptions and intensional contexts, a good read is the old but classic, *Names and Descriptions* by Leonard Linsky, as well as the Kripke book mentioned above.

Genus/Species Relations Between General Terms

General terms are often related in many ways but perhaps the most important relation is that of *genus* and *species*. As logicians use the terms 'genus' and 'species', they have no direct connection with their use in biology. In logic, a term A is said to be a genus of another term B when all the referents of B are referents of A but not vice-versa (that is, A has referents that B does not). In such a case, B is also said to be a species of A. So whenever A is a genus of B, B is thereby a species of A. For example, 'animal' is a genus of 'dog', 'cat', 'fish', 'lion', etc., while all of these terms are species of 'animal'.

Another way of putting this leans on a couple of very basic notions from mathematics, *subset* and *superset*. In mathematics, if one set is entirely contained in another, that is, all the members of the first set are members of the second, but not vice versa, then the first set is a subset of the second and the second is a superset of the first set. So as logicians use the term 'genus' and 'species', it is equivalent to that which mathematicians call 'superset' and 'subset'. To know the one is to know the other. Two notions for the price of one!

It should be clear that genus and species are, like so many terms of our language, relative terms. By that I mean that one and the same concept can be both a genus and a species, depending on what it is related to. For example, 'dog' is a genus when related to 'poodle', 'boxer' or 'collie' but is a species when related to 'animal'. (Similar to other relative terms like mother/daughter, father/son, boss/worker, etc., as we'll see in more detail in the chapter on fallacies). For now, some exercises.

Exercises

I. For each of the following general terms, identify the genus and the species and then provide two more species. Also, provide two referents of any of the concepts, either of those given or of the species you provide.

1. Dog, Animal
2. Baseball player, shortstop
3. Tiger, Cat
4. Vehicle, golf cart
5. Chalk, substance
6. Waterbed, Furniture
7. Textbook, book
8. Snow, Precipitation
9. Skill, juggling
10. Raspberries, Fruit

II. Identify at least three referents for each of the general terms below. After that, try to identify a genus and a species for each term as well.

1. Philosopher
2. Tree
3. Country
4. Artist
5. Number
6. River

III. Extend the list of species below.

1. Books: biographies, hardbacks, textbooks, . . .

2. Automobiles: red automobiles, expensive automobiles, . . .

3. Trees: backyard trees, maple, pine, . . .

4. Clothing: expensive clothing, clothing made by Oscar de la Renta, . . .

5. Games: board games, basketball games, . . .

Abstract/Concrete

A notion that is related to the genus/species relationship is that of *abstract* and *concrete*. The notion of being abstract, and its kin, abstraction, are important to logic. But the reason they are important to logic is because they are important to getting on in the world as well. Critics of logic notwithstanding, the fact is that logic attempts to codify and make precise various practices that comprise what we might call being rational. And one very important part of being rational is the ability to abstract from one's experience, to think in an abstract way. Since you are, by definition, a rational being, you are quite adept at abstracting, whether you know what that means or not. So what is abstraction, to put things as Socrates might?

Roughly speaking, and one can only speak roughly about such things, abstraction involves focusing on some aspects, parts, segments, etc., of our experience to the exclusion of other aspects, parts, segments, etc. And I trust we can agree that this is something that all of us do quite often and thus quite well. Indeed, if we could not do this, we simply would not be able to get on in this world. The most basic and fundamental case of abstraction is that which allows us to distinguish between objects, to distinguish one thing from another. When we first learned language at our parents' knees, each of us already had some vague sense of the differences between various items of our experience, items like tables, chairs, pets, people, items of clothing, cookies, books, crayons, hula hoops, etc. To appreciate that a purple hula hoop is a different object from an oatmeal cookie may not, as intellectual achievements go, be at the level of appreciating that $E = mc^2$, but it was a step in the right direction. More importantly, it is a very simple example of abstraction at work.

Oddly, when someone comes to recognize a table as being one thing or object, different from other objects, like a chair or a painting, s/he is abstracting but in doing so is also identifying particular objects. Particular objects that we encounter in our day to day life are concrete objects, by logic's lights, and such objects are the referents of general terms, the abstract terms of language. Thus, my wife is a concrete object, as am I, as is our coffee-maker, and so on. Of course, my wife is a referent of many general terms, including 'woman', 'mother', 'U.S. citizen', etc. But it's important to be able to appreciate the difference between the particular concrete objects that exist independently of our abstractions and the general terms that result from our abstracting activities.

Once we distinguish between one concrete object and another, the next move in the abstraction game involves appreciating various similarities between various concrete objects. Despite their many differences, a hula hoop and a cookie are similar in at least one respect, namely, each is round or circular. (Of course, there are many other similarities that would make sense to you only after some language was under your belt, like the fact that both the hoop and the cookie are made by humans, are less than 5,000 years old, are both members of the universe, etc.). And this particular similarity of being round or circular, nicely enough, can be found in other things nearby as well, things like plates and automobile wheels and bowls and clocks and records and golf balls and pots and pans and CDs, etc. Our abstracting abilities give rise to our seeing round and circular as a particular *property*, a property shared by all that have a round shape but not shared by books and sofas and 8 x 11 pieces of paper. But these other items could be said to have a different property, namely, the property of not being round. And one would have a very simple dichotomy for the things in one's environment, namely round things and non-round things. But the human ability to register similarities is quite prolific and very quickly leads to a host of other properties similar to round, like rectangular, square, oblong, not to mention red, yellow, blue, hard, soft, flexible, etc. In short, off we go.

One underappreciated aspect of abstraction is that it involves as much ignoring of properties and things as it does an appreciation of similarities of things. When we come to see wheels, hula hoops, golf balls and plates as all being round, not only are we appreciating the similar shape each of these items has but we are also ignoring the substance each is made of (rubber, plastic, urethane, china), their colors, smells, textures, etc. Focus on one thing (roundness, or more generally, shape) requires that one ignore other properties.

Another aspect of abstraction that deserves emphasis is that without it, language is impossible. As a result, it is often said, correctly by my lights, that every term of our language is abstract. Or, a bit more hyperbolically, that all language is metaphor. (This claim is often attributed to the philosopher Hannah Arendt but as far as I know, others may have said it as well.) It is clear that the act of creating terms of language requires the ability to abstract from one's experience. Inventing terms to stand for or represent things in the world is abstract thinking *par excellence*. As noted above, the very act of distinguishing one thing from another in our experiences is a case of abstraction. To distinguish an apple from an orange involves the ability to think abstractly. And the creation of different terms to mark and communicate that difference also involves abstraction. So anyone who is able to speak a language is, *ipso facto*, an abstract thinker.

Be this as it may, however, abstraction allows us to identify concrete objects, as well as enable us to see various sorts of similarities between concrete objects, and of course, ignoring what we regard as irrelevant differences, allows us to sort things into sets or collections based on those similarities. The concrete objects are identified by singular terms while the resulting collections are exactly what our general terms can, in part, be taken as designating. When we move from Fido, Rover and Spot to 'dog', and from 'dog' to 'mammal' and from 'mammal' to 'animal', we are playing the abstraction game.

The following amended example from S.I. Hayakawa's *Language in Thought and Action*, which is one he himself got from Korzybski, known as the abstraction ladder, illustrates nicely the abstraction component of our language.

Living thing

Animal

Mammal

Feline

Cat

Siamese cat

Fluffy

Type/Token

A common distinction in logic and related studies of language is that between *type* and *token*. The distinction is quite similar to that between a general term and its referents but not identical. The best example of the distinction, not surprisingly given its name, comes from the alphabet and its use in our language. Some inquiring minds wondered, for example, how many 'A's there are in, for example, the word 'away'. One plausible answer is, two. Another plausible answer is one, for there is *really* only one 'A' in the English language, although it gets used many, many times over and over again. Leaning on the old saying that where there is a contradiction, a distinction is needed, people distinguished between a type and its particular tokens. There is only one type but there can be endless tokens of it. So there is only one type 'A' in English but it can be copied over and over again as needed and the copies are called its tokens. The same distinction applies to newspapers. At the newsstand there are many copies, or tokens, of the morning newspaper but each copy is a token of a type from which each copy was printed.

Now if you think back to some of our examples of general terms and referents, we can appreciate that the referents of most general terms are not related as tokens are to types. My pet cat Pepper is a referent of the general term 'cat' but so too is Sabu, a Persian cat who lives next door. And they are quite different looking cats. No one would say the same about two copies of the morning newspaper. In fact, if my copy of the paper differed in any significant way from your copy, we would have our doubts that we had copies of the same paper. Given the type/token distinction, we can make sense of the claim that there is only one *Moby Dick*, only one *Godfather* movie, only one *Dark Side of the Moon*, etc., since each is a type that admits of many tokens. As such, we can cite titles of books, CDs, and movies as examples of referents of the general terms, 'book', 'CD', and 'movie', understanding the titles in the sense of a type rather than a token.

Thinking experiment – Some people balk at treating titles of books, movies, and recordings as ways of identifying referents. In defense of their position, they often cite automobile makes and models. It seems that no one would say that '65 Ford Galaxie' counts as a referent of 'car' (rather than a species) since there are clearly many, many cars that are 65 Ford Galaxies. And yet couldn't we see '65 Ford Galaxie' as a type and all of the various cars that are 65 Ford Galaxies as tokens thereof? Of course, it's our language and we can decide to talk as we please. But one difference between the movie case and the make/model case is that we know that the tokens of a movie, e.g., your copy of *Casablanca* and my copy, are, and must be, essentially identical in order to be copies of the same movie. A similar claim cannot, it seems, be said about my '65 Ford Galaxie and your '65 Ford Galaxie. What do you think?

Briefly reviewing, all general terms are the result of abstracting from the world of individuals. Although all individual things in the world are in some sense both unique and similar to lots of other things, we find it useful to lump individuals together based on some similarity or other between them. Think dogs and cats, trees, desks, students, tubas, rock groups, etc.

For me, the abstract character of general terms also means that a general term is our invention, our tool for classifying individuals into convenient classes so as to lend order to the blooming buzzing confusion that is our experience. Another aspect of the abstract is that it is not part of the natural world, that is, the world that exists independently of us. Prior to our language inventing, there was simply no such thing as the general term 'dog'. There were individual dogs, to be sure, but it was our propensity to organize, focus and ignore that created the general term for these concrete objects.

To further illustrate the difference between the abstract and the non-abstract, we can say that the concept 'dog', unlike individual dogs like Fido, Rover and Spot, cannot be petted, doesn't need feeding and cannot pee on your carpet. Abstract objects, in contrast to concrete items, are the sorts of things that are brought into existence by thought. They are, to make use of a popular but rather controversial distinction, invented rather than found in the natural world.

Although the two notions, abstract and concrete, have a variety of uses among logicians and language theorists, perhaps one simple point of agreement is that particular individual objects in the world are all deemed to be concrete objects. As noted above, concrete objects exist independently of humans and their language-creating activities. Thus, Fido is a concrete object, as are JFK and Jon Stewart. However, some logicians speak quite unabashedly of concrete general terms and abstract general terms. (A manner of speaking that has its merits–see, for example, W.V. Quine's *From a Logical Point of View*). For our purposes, we will say that a genus is always more abstract (less concrete) than any of its species and a species is always less abstract (more concrete) than any genus of which it is a species. We will also say that the referents of singular terms are all concrete objects and that all concrete objects can be named, that is, can be the referent of a singular term.

Exercises

I. Arrange the following terms in order of most concrete to most abstract. If you think the relations between some of the terms allow for alternative arrangements, feel free to say why and to offer those alternatives.

1. Doctor of medicine, plastic surgeon, surgeon, professional person
2. Parallelogram, polygon, square, rectangle, quadrilateral
3. Flavored corn chips, snack food, Doritos, corn chips, food
4. Minnesota Vikings, professional sports team, NFL team, NFL teams that haven't won a Super Bowl, sports team
5. Entertainer George Clooney, actor, human
6. Spaniel, living thing, dog, mammal, Cocker spaniel, animal
7. Trilateral figure, triangle, figure, right triangle
8. Durable goods, GE refrigerator, appliance, human artifact
9. Brother, family member, sibling, kin
10. Monopoly, Dot.com monopoly, games, board games, activities

---

Increasing intension – A fairly straightforward, and quite reliable relationship exists between the addition of intensional content to general terms and a decrease in the number of things the resulting term applies to. More simply, the more terms one adds to some general term, the result is an increasingly less abstract, more concrete term. For example, if we start with the general term 'dog', we might add a bit of intensional content by amending the term 'black' to it. The resulting term, 'black dog' will pick out a smaller class of things than 'dog' itself. For all black dogs are dogs but not vice-versa. (However, for a rather famous challenge to this seemingly obvious claim, there is a rather notorious dispute among Chinese philosophers concerning whether a white horse is a horse or not. For details see *Disputers of the Tao*, by Angus Graham. The dispute also gets a mention in many other texts on Chinese philosophy). If we continue adding terms, for example, 'over two years of age', 'playful', 'cute', 'likes to chase cars', etc., the addition of each term further narrows the class of things we are talking about. The moral seems clear then, increase the intension and we decrease the class of things referred to, that is, we get a decrease in abstractness.

Of course, it doesn't take much effort to find weird counterexamples to this moral. But they are somewhat stilted, to put it mildly. All one needs to do to find cases where increasing intension fails to decrease the abstractness is to think of intensions that simply do not apply to any objects other than those which the original term applied to. As an example, consider the following case, which is a slight variation to one offered in Copi and Cohen's *Introduction to Logic*:

Start with the term, 'living person', add on 'less than 5,000 years old', and add to this, 'who has never set foot on Pluto', and it is clear we end up increasing the intension but leaving the abstractness, understood in terms of genus/species relations between the three terms, unaffected. The three terms have the same extension.

II. Provide a genus for each of these concepts and then provide a genus for the first genus.

1. Golf cart, bus, sports car
2. Chopsticks, spoon, ladle
3. Bengal tiger, snow leopard, lion
4. Loud, soft, harmonious
5. Violin, cello, Stradivarius violin
6. Earth, fire, water
7. Table, desk, chair

III. A good exercise, and one that is probably similar to those you may have done in English Comp class, is to start with a sentence and then alter it, step by step, by changing some of it terms to a corresponding genus or species. For example, suppose we start with the sentence: The quick brown fox jumped over the lazy dog.
We can substitute 'mammal' for 'fox', as fox is a species of mammal, to get,
The quick brown mammal jumped over the lazy dog.
We could get more specific by substituting 'bulldog' for 'dog', as 'dog' is its genus, to get: The quick brown mammal jumped over the lazy bulldog.
Since 'hopping' can be considered a species of 'jumping', we could get,
The quick brown mammal hopped over the lazy bulldog, and so on.
If you find this sort of thing fun, here are some starting sentences that you can alter to your heart's delight by changing some of their terms to their respective genus or species as you see fit. Enjoy.

1. She came a long way from St. Louie.
2. Gottlob Frege learned the laws of thought from George Boole.
3. The Twins defeated the Cardinals in seven games in the '87 World Series.
4. Lions and tigers and bears, oh my.
5. There is more than one way to skin a cat.
6. The bellhop threw the luggage on the floor and walked quickly out of the room.
7. Somewhere over the rainbow, bluebirds fly.
8. If you need a new car, call Jones Ford today.
9. Now is a good time to buy a new house.
10. Animals sweat, men perspire and women glisten.

Organizing Concepts/Classification

Perhaps the easiest way to learn the basic do's and don'ts of organization and classification is to see a case where the do's and don'ts have been ignored and violated. So consider the following hypothetical scheme for organizing CDs, which consists of the following 10 categories.

CD collection
1. Favorite road trip CDs
2. CDs containing songs written by J. J. Cale
3. CDs with interesting cover art
4. CDs released after 1999
5. Bob Dylan CDs
6. CDs I'll never listen to again
7. CDs with broken or cracked covers
8. CDs my first wife bought for me
9. CDs bought at *Ernie November*
10. CDs that cost me less than $50

That is, suppose someone has 10 plastic bins, each bin containing one of the labels above on it. Obviously, there would be trouble if someone were to attempt to use this scheme for organizing his/her CDs, not to mention using it to help locate a particular CD. We can appreciate that it's quite likely that at least one Bob Dylan CD might also be among this person's favorite road trip CDs. If such were the case, the person would have at least two different bins in his/her scheme for the same CD. This problem is known as the problem of overlapping categories and it is definitely to be avoided in any viable organizing scheme. (although, there are some exceptions). And although the scheme has 10 categories, it may nonetheless be the case that some CDs in this collection in question simply do not fit into any of these particular categories. For example, Barry Manilow's *Singin' with the Big Bands* may fail to go into any of the categories mentioned–not a good thing. In short, we want to make sure that we have exactly one bin for each and every CD in the collection.

Another connection with mathematics. In mathematics, such a scheme of organization, where there is exactly one place for each thing to be classified, is known as a *partition*.

Simply put, a logical classification, like a partition from mathematics, will have categories that are mutually exclusive and jointly exhaustive. Below we will see what philosophers have offered as ways to ensure that we get mutually exclusive and jointly exhaustive categories for our classification schemes.

Another traditional component of a logical classification, going back at least to Plato, is that the creation of the categories for a group of things should focus on important or fundamental properties of the things involved. Perhaps the paradigmatic case of categorization involves the general term, 'animal'. Now a child might suggest that we could classify animals by color, so we could have categories like red animals, blue animals, green animals, brown animals, etc. While we could certainly create such a scheme, and ensure that it is mutually exclusive and jointly exhaustive, such a scheme would not have satisfied Plato. For such a scheme would not be based on important or essential traits of the animals. Instead, it would focus on the rather superficial and unimportant property of color. To appreciate Plato's worry, consider that a black poodle and a white poodle would belong in different categories, while zebras and penguins would belong in the same one. Not a happy result.

Of course, we can also appreciate that the properties of things that are important or essential in some particular group of things can vary, according to the purposes for which the classification scheme is to be used. So we can relax Plato's principle a bit and say that a good scheme should use properties that one deems important, where what is deemed important is connected to the use of the classification. Thus, if one is thinking about having animals in one's backyard that will go well with the color scheme of one's house then one may very well classify animals according to color. But if one is trying to categorize animals according to key biological similarities, one's categories are likely to be those that are similar to the ones used by biologists and zoologists, namely, mammal, reptile, cold-blooded, warm-blooded, egg-laying, live birth, etc.

I mentioned above that there is a fairly simple way of ensuring that a classification scheme comes out with mutually exclusive and jointly exhaustive categories. The way to do this is to choose an *organizing principle*, which serves to ensure that the resulting categories do not overlap. For example, suppose that you wish to provide a classification of clothing. Now there are many organizing principles one might choose for generating categories for the classification. One easy way to find a principle is to think of how manufacturers and retailers of clothing organize clothing. Many clothing manufacturers will use the principle of **material**, which naturally generates categories like 'natural', 'synthetic', or 'cotton', 'wool', 'nylon', etc. Retailers use a wide variety of principles, including **size**, which yields the categories 'small', 'medium', 'large', etc., **gender**, yielding the categories 'male, 'female', 'unisex', **age**, yielding the categories 'infants', 'children', 'teens', 'adults', **designer**, yielding the categories 'Gucci', 'Armani', 'Oscar De La Renta', and finally, **price/cost**, yielding the categories '$20 and under, '$21 to 50', 'above $50'. Notice that once you choose a principle to guide your classification hand, it is relatively easy to find categories that are mutually exclusive. If you mix principles in your category making, the result is usually a series of overlapping categories.

Some hints about principles that you might find useful. First, for many of the things that we encounter in this world, they typically have a function. (Greek philosophers loved to use the functions of things to help them understand the world. Aristotle even said that human beings have a function and that function is what he called "activity of the soul", or thinking, but that is a matter for a course in ethics). As such, function is often a handy principle to use in generating categories for some group of objects. Indeed, it is likely that when one thinks of the most common categories associated with a group of objects, those categories are tied to the principle of function. For example, if one is asked to identify categories of clothing, one readily thinks of categories like shoes, pants, shirts, skirts, dresses, etc. These categories are, by my lights, generated by appeal to the principle, function. Another tip is that when one is considering groups of objects that are bought and sold, which encompasses a great many things, a useful principle is cost/price. Finally, a fairly all-purpose principle is one that appeals to language, namely, alphabetical order. We often find it convenient to classify objects by appeal to the terms by which we call them. So if we are given the class of vegetables, we could classify them by alphabetical order as follows: Vegetables from A to F, Vegetables from G to M, Vegetables from M to Z, or some other alphabetical ordering.

First Logic

Exercises

I. For each of the following classifications, determine whether the classification consists of mutually exclusive and jointly exhaustive categories, and then determine the principle (or principles) of the classification and say whether you think it is or could be an essential or fundamental property of the things being classified.

1. Careers: successful, rewarding, demanding, low paying, journalist
2. Automobiles: 4-cylinder, 6-cylinder, 8-cylinder
3. Sports: professional, amateur, baseball, played indoors
4. Clothing: hats, shirts, skirts, pants, casual, low-cost
5. Television shows: drama, situation comedy, reality, news, Emmy-award winning, adult programming
6. Books: academic, audio, reference, fiction, *N.Y. Times* best sellers
7. Dinners: take-out, Chinese, low-cost, quick and easy, nutritious, tasty

II. Go back to the classifications in the previous exercise and, where appropriate, try to identify the different principles that are at work in the schemes that have overlapping categories. Next, choose one of your identified principles and then compose a classification scheme based on that principle. Rinse and repeat.

III. Provide as many principles as you can think of for generating categories for each of the following classes of objects.
1. Books
2. Cars
3. Food
4. Bodies of water
5. Careers
6. Jewelry
7. Furniture
8. Sports

IV. Order each of the following sets of concepts. In each set, some are at the same level of abstraction and some are not. Fill in concepts where you see fit.

1. Mammals, trees, granite, pumice, flowers, amphibians

2. Baptist, Methodist, Jewish, Religions, Catholic, Islam, Shiite

3. Public universities, Big Ten schools, University of Minnesota, MNSCU schools, St. Cloud State, Minnesota State University, Mankato

4. CD player, audio equipment, CDs, wall speakers, receivers

5. Philosophy, Ethics, ethical theories, Utilitarianism, Deontology, Emotivism

Increasing intension

A fairly straightforward, and quite reliable relationship exists between the addition of intensional content to general terms and a decrease in the number of things the resulting term applies to. More simply, the more terms one adds to some general term, the result is an increasingly less abstract, more concrete term. For example, if we start with the general term 'dog', we might add a bit of intensional content by amending the term 'black' to it. The resulting term, 'black dog', will pick out a smaller class of things than 'dog' itself. For all black dogs are dogs but not vice-versa. (However, for a rather famous challenge to this seemingly obvious claim, there is a rather notorious dispute among Chinese philosophers concerning whether a white horse is a horse or not. For details see *Disputers of the Tao*, by Angus Graham. The dispute also gets a mention in many other texts on Chinese philosophy.) If we continue adding terms, for example, 'over two years of age', 'playful', 'cute', 'likes to chase cars', etc., the addition of each term further narrows the class of things we are talking about. The moral seems clear then, increase the intension and we decrease the class of things referred to, that is, we get a decrease in abstractness.

Of course, it doesn't take much effort to find weird counterexamples to this moral. But they are somewhat stilted, to put it mildly. All one needs to do to find cases where increasing intension fails to decrease the abstractness is to think of intensions that simply do not apply to any objects other than those which the original term applied to. As an example, consider the following case, which is a slight variation to one offered in Copi and Cohen's *Introduction to Logic*:

> Start with the term, 'living person', add on 'less than 5,000 years old', and add to this, 'who has never set foot on Pluto', and it is clear we end up increasing the intension but leaving the abstractness, understood in terms of genus/species relations between the three terms, unaffected. The three terms have the same extension.

Chapter 3: Definitions

We learn the meanings of practically all our words . . . not from dictionaries, not from definitions, but from hearing these [words] as they accompany actual situations in life and learning to associate certain [words] with certain situations.
S.I. Hayakawa, *Language in Thought and Action*

To define an expression is, paradoxically speaking, to explain how to get along without it. To define is to eliminate.
W.V. Quine, *Quiddities*

Things had essences, for Aristotle, but only linguistic forms have meaning. Meaning is what essence becomes when it is divorced from the object of reference and wedded to the word.
W.V. Quine, "Two Dogmas of Empiricism"

At some point in their language-using life (often after being exposed to a second language), most language-users come to realize that the words of human languages are quite arbitrary. That is, we all realize that there is nothing about 'cat' that makes it a better or worse label for cats than many other terms. We could have used 'tove' rather than 'cat' to name our feline friends, and the same goes for all of our general terms, not to mention proper names. Just as a rose, by another name, would smell as sweet, William Shakespeare, by another name, would have written as well.

Of course, nothing reveals this arbitrariness better than recalling that different languages, French, German, Spanish, etc., each use different words to refer to the common objects of our world. The French use 'chat' to speak of cats, the Spanish use 'gato', while the Germans use 'Katze'. It is silly to say that one of these terms is the correct term for talking about cats. Any word will do but it is important to choose one and stick with it. As many a philosopher has noted, names and words are arbitrary but once chosen must be adhered to, in order to avoid linguistic chaos. Of course, once we have decided on certain terms for certain kinds of objects, this limits our freedom to create new words, at least if we keep ease and utility in mind. If our goal is confusion and disutility, we could simply create new words each day, depending on how we felt like speaking. A wonderful example of the problems engendered by deciding to be arbitrary in language use is Humpty Dumpty in Lewis Carroll's *Alice in Wonderland*, who stuns Alice by claiming that he is free to use language any way he wishes.

Since English already has its oldest and oft-used terms in place, our freedom to create new terms and meanings for them via definitions is quite limited. This also means that the vast majority of definitions that we can offer for English terms are ones that can be said to be correct or incorrect. Although getting a definition right, that is, having it match customary usage, is an important consideration, more important questions are whether the definition is instructive, clear, covers the right objects, isn't circular, and the like. That is, just like almost everything else to do with logic, formal considerations, even in the case of definitions, take precedence over matters of content. A good definition of a common word in our language must correspond, in some sense, with standard usage but it will be judged better or worse in large part on the basis of its satisfying various formal constraints.

Before looking at some of the do's and don'ts of good definitions, a couple of distinctions will come in handy in this chapter and elsewhere in logic.

USE/MENTION
Logicians mark the distinction between *using* a word and *mentioning* it by using single quote marks. The single quote marks are a way of naming the thing in the quotes. To see how and why this works, consider the following sentences:

1. Pepper is my favorite cat.
2. Pepper is a two-syllable word.

It's clear that if 'Pepper' were used in the same way in both sentences, one of the sentences would be nonsense. My cat is not a two-syllable word and the name of my cat is not my favorite cat. To make sense of the sentences, we use 'Pepper' in the first sentence to do its usual job of naming my cat, while in the second sentence, we should put single quote marks around the name of my cat to form a name of it, allowing us to say correctly that it, namely, the thing in the quotes, is a two-syllable word. Properly amended, we get the following:

1. Pepper is my favorite cat.
2. 'Pepper' is a two-syllable word.

Keep this distinction in mind as we look at what logicians say about definitions. (Sharp-eyed readers may have noticed the use/mention distinction at work in the previous chapter, as well.)

DEFINIENDUM AND DEFINIENS
It is convenient to distinguish between the word or expression that we are defining and the word or expression that serves as our definition. Philosophers have offered *definiendum* as a fancy term for the term we are defining and *definiens* as an equally fancy term for the definition itself. So if we wish to define 'human being', we would say that this expression is our definiendum and if our proposed definition is 'rational animal', this expression would be our definiens.

What is definition?
Socrates, philosophy's patron saint, went around asking his fellow Athenians questions like, "What is virtue?", "What is friendship?", "What is courage?".

According to most philosophers, Socrates was asking people to define these terms. But it seems safe to say that Socrates wasn't asking people to tell him what the dictionary says about these terms. It seems safe to say that Socrates was giving voice to what most of us do ourselves. For all of us, at some time or another, are led to ask, "What is love?", "What is good?", "What is right?", etc. And more recently, we have been led to ask ourselves questions like, "What is art?", "What is democracy?", "What is pornography?" In each of these cases, it seems that people are interested in knowing something about the world rather than simply knowing how a word is used. In short, these questions reveal that people want to improve, in some way or other, on the standard use of the terms in question. And often, such improvement is called for, in both philosophy and science.

The philosopher W.V. Quine, in his book *Quiddities*, which Quine himself calls "an intermittently philosophical dictionary", draws a distinction between defining an expression and defining objects or things in the world. Quine sees this distinction as giving us an object-directed notion of definition and a term-directed notion. Quine rightly notes that when we are puzzled more about the objects and things than we are about the use of an expression, we are probably interested in the object-directed definition. And vice-versa. And yet, as Quine notes, the object-directed definition reduces to the term-directed definition because we define things by defining the terms that refer to the things. Thus, we define numbers by defining 'number' and define art by defining 'art'.

Quine fails to note, however, that it may prove very difficult to get those who seem to have different ideas about, for example, art, to agree about the definition of 'art'. So perhaps we can say that a satisfactory definition of some controversial term like 'art', is one that makes clear what one counts as art and what one does not but which doesn't stray too terribly far from ordinary usage of the term. If we seek a definition of controversial terms that will resolve all disagreements connected with the term, we are probably never going to find one. Nor should we expect to. With a term like 'art', we should expect there to be disagreements about whether particular creations are or are not art. And we should not take such disagreements as proof that one or the other of the parties to the dispute doesn't really understand the meaning of 'art'. We should no more seek to solve all disagreements about art by a definition than we should seek to make everyone like oysters by changing the definition of 'oyster'.

Officially speaking, definitions define words/symbols, not things in the world. So we define 'shoe' but not the things on your feet. This official line leads some to hold that definitions are rather trivial things, since the way we speak, as noted above, seems a rather arbitrary affair. But we ought not be fooled by the official story into thinking that definitions are simply about language use. A bit of reflection reveals that how we define our terms does much to tell us about things in the world, since it is things in the world that our terms are about. Still, it is important to know when we are talking about the words of our language and when we are talking about the world and its objects. It is also good to keep in mind that our knowledge of the words of our language, or better, our knowledge of what the terms of our language mean, is not exact knowledge, is not precise knowledge. Most of us have a workable understanding of the great majority of the words we use in our daily lives. We know, in short, enough about the term to be credited as being someone who knows what the term means. As Quine likes to put it, most of us understand our terms well enough to use that term to "facilitate our negotiations in the language". And part of that facility involves being able to assess suggestions for using the term in question, that is, proposed definitions.

Consider a wonderful example of this sort of facility from the philosopher William James in the opening lecture of his book *Pragmatism*. One of the most wonderful aspects of this example is that it involves an expression of English that every English speaker would likely claim to know the meaning of, namely, 'going around'. The term, or better expression, 'going around' is hardly controversial. That is, few of us have ever had our use of this expression challenged by other competent speakers, in large part because we usually agree on how the expression is used and ought to be used. It is small wonder then that James resorts to a thought experiment in order to bring out a case in which our use of this expression might differ.

Someone in James' camping party has imagined a scenario in which a squirrel is on all fours on the trunk of a tree and a man is directly across from the squirrel on the other side of the tree, facing it. We are then to imagine that the man circles the tree in one direction and as he does so, the squirrel moves on the tree in unison with the man. It's as if the man and the squirrel are connected to the ends of a rod between them that is moving in a circular fashion. And the question is asked: Is the man going around the squirrel? Most of my students say that the man is not going around the squirrel. A few say he is. In his story, James says the members of his camping party were divided evenly on the matter. (Frankly, I find this hard to believe, but it is James' story after all.)

To resolve the disagreement, James offers two definitions, each of which has the virtue of being precise enough to allow us to say one of them is satisfied in this case while the other is not. I will save the proposed definitions for a class session. But perhaps you can think of some definitions that might work. Give it a try. Anyway, James concludes that deciding who is correct about whether the man goes around the squirrel is the relatively simple matter of deciding which definition of 'going around' to use.

Many of us no doubt worry that who is correct here seems to rest simply on the rather arbitrary decision of which definition to use. Shouldn't we, couldn't we, ask whether one of the definitions is preferable and then try to defend our claims with reason and argument? At this point, I will say only that this is a legitimate enough worry but that I will not pause to discuss it further.

Although philosophers and logicians have distinguished a wide variety of kinds of definitions, we will focus on one of the more ancient forms of definitions and one that chimes in well with the notions introduced in the previous chapter, namely *genus and differentia* definitions.

Marks of a Good Genus/Differentia Definition
1. Provides a genus and differentia
2. Does not include the definiendum in the definiens (that is, is not circular)
3. The definiens and the definiendum pick out the same class of objects/things (make sure that the definition is neither too broad nor too narrow or accidentally overlapping)
4. Provides the "important" attributes of the general term's referents
5. Is reasonably clear, precise and literal
6. Is affirmative rather than negative (says what the definiendum means rather than what it does not mean)

Exercises

I. Identify any problems in the following definitions. As always, if a definition is too broad or too narrow, provide a counterexample.

1. COMPUTER: an electronic instrument that has replaced the typewriter

2. GOVERNMENT: an institution that levies taxes on its subjects

3. BREVITY: the soul of wit

4. RAIN BOOTS: outer clothing made of rubber that repels water

5, PENCIL: a writing instrument that has an eraser

6. ART: whatever is hanging in art museums

7. POLITICS: the science that studies the economic behavior of people in society

8. NET: anything made with interstitial vacuities

9. CAMEL: ship of the desert

10. BELIEF: the demi-cadence which closes a musical phrase in the symphony
        of our intellectual life

11. NOISE: any unwanted signal

12. WEED: anything that you don't want growing in your garden

13. HARMONY: the absence of discord

14. THEIST: someone who is not an atheist or an agnostic

15. CONSERVATIVE: a person who is opposed to gay marriage and taxes

II. Say which of our marks of a good definition (other than 3) are violated by the
following definitions.

1. CONFIDENT: an attribute of people who are secure in their own skin

2. ART: the stored honey of the human soul

3. SEVEN: the number of deadly sins

4. SCIENCE: self-conscious common sense

5. PIETY: a virtue consisting of service and devotion to one's god

6. POVERTY: the economic condition in which one is not rich

7. COLOR: an effluvium from shapes that is directed to the eyes

8. JUSTICE: when you do what is right according to your community

9. GOOD: knowledge of the good

10. EDIBLE: anything that is not inedible

Chapter 4: Declarative Sentences – The World of Truth and Falsity

The world is all that is the case.   Ludwig Wittgenstein

Logic chases truth up the tree of grammar.   W.V. Quine, *Philosophy of Logic*

Aristotle's famous account of speaking truly and falsely goes more or less as follows:

> To say of what is that it is, and of what is not that it is not, is to speak truly.
> And to say of what is that it is not and to say of what is not that it is, is to
> speak falsely.

Although this famous saying is more praiseworthy for its brevity than its clarity, it nonetheless gives an account of speaking truly and falsely worth keeping in mind. In this chapter, we will put our terms, general and singular, to work in helping us say things that can be regarded as being true or false, that is, saying things about the world that go beyond naming and classifying. In order to do this we need, in a word, sentences.

Truth be told, there are many kinds of sentences in English, many different ways of expressing our thoughts. But not all sentences allow us to speak truly and falsely. The common name for the sentences that do purport to say something true or false is *declarative sentences*. (*Fact-stating sentences* will also do to refer to such sentences.) As for those sentences whose job is something other than stating how things are, a standard list of such sentences includes *interrogatives*, e.g., "Is today Tuesday?", or "What are you wearing tonight?"; *imperatives* or *commands*, e.g., "Do your homework now", or "Close the door"; *expressive* or *emotive* sentences, "Hurray for the Twins", or "Go Vikings", among others. Couple these sorts of sentences with non-literal uses of sentences, including the ironical, metaphorical and sarcastic, and it is clear that on many, many occasions, sentences of our language are doing something other than setting out our claims about what is true or false.

In this chapter and beyond, we will focus, as is customary in logic, on declarative sentences. But we will also have to go beyond them and speak about their use on some particular occasion and in some particular context or other. For a sentence is typically identified in terms of its syntactic and formal features, and such a characterization often fails to do justice to its semantic features. Simply put, the same sentence can be used to say different things by different people on different occasions.

> **Syntax** -- the part of language analysis that focuses on the formal and physical properties of symbols in dealing with the formation of words, phrases and sentences; in particular, the syntactical properties of words and sentences can be studied quite readily without knowing anything at all about what they mean.
>
> **Semantics** -- that part of language analysis that focuses on the relation between signs/symbols and what they represent or mean; since these things are typically things in the world, semantics, in distinction from syntax, involves word-world relations.

To see this, take a simple sentence like, "I forgot to go to work today". It is clear that we want to allow that two different people, with two different jobs, can utter this very sentence on different days. Of course, because of the personal pronoun, 'I' and the temporal term, 'today', and their connection with the term 'work', the sentence will mean something different when uttered by different people with different jobs on different days. That is, semantically, two different people with different jobs uttering this sentence on different days would rightly be understood to have said different things. Both persons would say the same thing about themselves but it would be different selves about which they speak, and a different thing forgotten, and so on.

Because of considerations like this, (if you think the problem is easily avoided, think of sentences like, 'the war is over', 'the king is dead', 'the paper has come', etc.), it is necessary to distinguish sentences from their various uses on different occasions by different people. A common way of speaking of a sentence's use on some occasion is to invoke the notion of a *statement*. A statement is a sentence that we imagine being used by someone on some occasion in a particular context. As such, two different people uttering the same sentence typically yields two different statements.

But now what about the opposite phenomenon? That is, what about the possibility of two people using different declarative sentences and yet saying the same thing, meaning the same thing? Can two people use different declarative sentences to make the same statement? Although there are some who balk at this idea, it seems clear that different declarative sentences can be used by different people to make statements that are identical in meaning. Perhaps the simplest case of this would involve people speaking different languages.

The following three sentences are not even in the same language, yet it seems clear that they say the same thing about our world.

1. La neige est blanche.
2. Der schnee ist weiss.
3. Snow is white.

Of course, we don't have to imagine sentences from different languages to illustrate this possibility. We can get the same statement from different sentences by replacing some of the terms of a sentence by synonyms. Thus:

1. The cat is on the sofa.
2. The cat is on the couch.
3. The tabby is on the sofa.

Another way to get the same statement from different sentences is by varying the word order or grammatical construction of the statement. Thus:

1. The Cardinals won the Series.
2. The Series was won by the Cardinals.
3. Won by the Cardinals was the Series. (A poetical account of the victory).

Some important ground rules about declarative sentences

As just noted, when we speak of declarative sentences we typically have in mind the use of such a sentence in a particular context, that is, we imagine that someone is using the declarative sentence in question. We will also suppose that the statement is being offered sincerely and literally, that is, to make a statement that the speaker regards as stating the truth. We will, in short, suppose that the statement maker is committed to his/her statement being true. Following Gottlob Frege's lead, we will call such statements, *assertions*. To assert a declarative sentence is to utter or write a sentence that one is committed to being true.

It is time to set out some basic facts about declarative sentences and the assertions we make via their use. Some of these facts have already been discussed above and some have not. But in order to keep things tidy, the list below will prove useful.

1. Declarative sentences/statements purport to be either true or false.

2. Complete declarative sentences/statements contain at least a subject term and a predicate term (but usually contain much more); single terms are unable, except in odd cases, to express a complete thought/to state a fact.

3. To assert a sentence/statement is to claim that it is true, or to be committed to it being true.

4. Two or more declarative sentences can assert the same statement (or, if you prefer, can mean the same thing).

5. A single sentence can contain more than one declarative sentence/statement via the use of terms like 'and', 'or', 'if-then', 'but', 'although', 'believes', 'knows', etc. We will call sentences that contain more than one declarative sentence, *compound sentences*. We will call the sentences contained in compound sentences, *component sentences*.

6. A single sentence with component sentences may assert all of those component sentences or none of them, or any number in between. It is important to be able to distinguish the component sentences that are asserted from those that are not, since this marks the difference between sentences a speaker is committed to being true from those to which s/he is not so committed.

Asserting Compound and Component Sentences

In the case of basic compound sentences, that is, sentences containing terms like 'and', 'or', 'if-then', and their informal relatives, 'unless', 'but', 'although', etc., it is important to know when the assertion of the compound sentence commits one to asserting its component sentences. In some cases, the assertion of a compound sentence commits the person asserting it to the assertion of all of its parts and sometimes it does not. In order to be able to properly assess the claims and arguments of others, knowing how to determine which component sentences are asserted and which are not, is an indispensable skill. Since all indispensable skills are worth mastering, let's try to master this skill.

The rules governing the assertion or non-assertion of component sentences are fairly straightforward and, like many other rules of logic, are intimately linked to grammatical rules. For this reason, once you learn a few of the basic rules, the innate universal grammar in your head takes over and you can quite readily extend the basic rules to more complex cases. The simplest and most consistent of the rules for assertion of component sentences concern statements which make use of key logical terms, especially the terms, 'or', 'and' and 'if-then'.

Each of these fundamental logical terms can be used to create a compound declarative sentence by taking two declarative sentences and connecting them together via the use of one or more of these terms. Consider the following sentences:

1. The Cardinals lost today.
2. I'm out $100.
3. The Cardinals won today.

From these sentences, we could create an endless number of compound sentences using our logical connectives. For example, from 1 and 2, we can get the compound statement: If the Cardinals lost today then I'm out $100. We could get much the same sentence by putting together, 'The Cardinals won today' with 'I'm out $100' via the use of 'or', to get: Either the Cardinals won today or I'm out $100. Finally, we could use 1 and 2 and 'and' to get the pitiful: The Cardinals lost today and I'm out $100.

As competent English speakers, you no doubt have intuitions about which of the component sentences in the sentences above are asserted and which are not. Nonetheless, it's best to make these intuitions explicit.

Let's start with the if-then statement:

If the Cardinals lost today then I'm out $100.

All 'if-then' statements will contain at least two component sentences, one between the 'if' and 'then' and one following the 'then'. (Those that contain more than two sentences will come up in the exercises below. Also, in the next chapter we will consider alternative ways of expressing if-then sentences.) Now assuming that the original sentence is asserted (something that we will always do in assertion exercises), we are interested in whether either of these component sentences is being asserted. Since asserting a sentence is to commit to its truth, the question we need to ask is whether someone who asserts the entire 'if-then' statement is thereby committed to the truth of either of its component sentences, 'the Cardinals lost today', or 'I'm out $100'. Any component sentence that a speaker is committed to being true by asserting the entire sentence is also asserted.

In this particular case, it should be clear that asserting the 'if-then' statement does not commit one to the truth of either of the component sentences. After all, one would most likely assert the sentence above when one is uncertain of the outcome of the game in question. As such, one is not going to be committed to the truth of the claim, 'the Cardinals lost today'. Similarly, if one is not sure of the outcome of the game, one is equally unsure about being out $100. Thus, one is also not going to be committed to the truth of the sentence, 'I'm out $100'.

More formally, we can say that since 'if-then' statements can be true even when both of their component sentences are false, asserting an if-then statement *does not* result in the component sentences being asserted.

One more point. The nice thing about this case (as well as a nice example of a common characteristic of logic) is that it is not simply an accidental fact about this particular 'if-then' statement. For the same analysis can be applied to any 'if-then' statements. As with much else in logic, learn one case and you learn much. In particular, we do not have to concern ourselves with the particular content of 'if-then' statements. Once we identify a sentence as an asserted 'if-then' statement, we know that its component sentences are not asserted by someone who asserts the entire statement.

As far as the terms, 'or' and 'and' go, do you have any thoughts about whether or which of the component sentences of typical 'or' statements and typical 'and' statements are asserted? For that matter, what about sentences conjoined by the following terms?

because, since, after, before, even though, but

(NOTE: The first four terms in this list are not truth-functional connectives, while the last two are pretty much identical to a truth-functional use of 'and'. Do you agree?)

Other connectives worth considering are:

When, whenever, while, where, wherever

Propositional Attitudes
Many terms in our language stand for attitudes that we can take toward sentences and statements (among other things, of course), including terms like 'believe', 'know', 'suspect', 'realize', etc. Similarly, we can report on the attitudes others have toward various statements, including what they say, argue, prove, acknowledge, etc., about those statements. Because these terms are typically connected to sentences or statements, it's important to understand their effects on the assertion of component sentences.

Suppose that I assert the following sentence:

Bob believes that Robin Williams is the funniest man alive.

We can analyze this as follows:

X believes that p

where 'X' stands for the subject 'Bob' and 'p' stands for the sentence, 'Robin Williams is the funniest man alive'. For us, the key issue is the status of the component sentence, 'Robin Williams is the funniest man alive', namely is it asserted in this case or not? This question is to be decided by considering the way the propositional attitude 'believes' works. If we make an assertion about someone's belief, it seems clear that this does not commit us to asserting the sentence that follows it, the sentence that reports the content of another's belief.

Otherwise, we would be unable to report on another's belief unless we happened to agree with it and wanted to tell others that we were committed to its truth.

In contrast, suppose I assert the following sentence:

Church leaders acknowledge that Mother Teresa had a lifelong crisis of faith.

This sentence can be analyzed as above. Letting 'X' stand for the subject term of the sentence, namely, 'Church leaders', and letting 'p' stand for 'Mother Teresa had a lifelong crisis of faith', we get:

X acknowledges that p.

But now what about 'p'? Is it asserted in this case? The answer is YES. If you assert that someone acknowledges that 'p', you are not merely claiming something about X's attitude but you are also asserting that 'p' is true. It makes no sense to speak of someone acknowledging 'p' if 'p' is not true.

Simply put, whether the component sentences that follow a propositional attitude word are asserted or not is entirely a function of the particular propositional attitude word that precedes it. Most of the time, your English intuitions will suffice to decide the matter. When you are stumped, however, the usual technique of asking yourself whether the truth of the asserted sentence commits its speaker to the truth of the component sentence, should be used.

Some common propositional attitudes words include:

1. "opine that"
2. "glad that"
3. "regret that"
4. "approve that"
5. "disapprove that"
6. "hope that"
7. "fear that"
8. "command that"
9. "request that"
10. "forbid that"
11. "doubt that"
12. "know that"
13. "imagine that"
14. "say that"
15. "hear that"
16. "infer that"
17. "convinced that"

18. "recognize that"
19. "dream that"
20. "acknowledge that"
21. "aware that"
22. "argue that"
23. "suspect that"
24. "realize that"
25. "prove that"

Relative clauses

Many sentences contain what grammarians call relative clauses. Relative clauses contain a relative pronoun (who, whom, which, that) and a predicate expression. The relative pronoun's meaning is derived from another term of the sentence. Sometimes the relative clause asserts something about the subject of the sentence that is distinct from what the remainder of the sentence says about it. When it does so, a relative clause statement can be said to make two different assertions about the same subject. In other cases, the relative clause serves to add specificity to the subject of the sentence. When this happens, the sentence typically consists of a single assertion about the subject. Can you think of any examples of statements involving relative clauses that illustrate such differences? If not, you can find a few in the exercises.

The importance of proper comma use

A consideration of relative clause statements and their effects on what is or what is not asserted in a sentence reveals the importance of commas. Commas have the power to alter the meaning of sentences without adding or deleting any words in the sentences. The title of a fairly recent, and surprisingly best-selling book by Lynne Truss called, *Eats, Shoots, & Leaves*, also illustrates the importance of commas. (Can you see how removing some of the commas might alter the meaning of the title?) Much of Truss' book is devoted to scolding the linguistically unfussy among us about our lax attitude about language use, and commas come in for extra attention.

Another nice, and somewhat humorous, example of the importance of commas comes when one takes well-known passages from literature and alters them by adding or removing commas as the case may be. As a starting point, I'll mention the example I like best, the opening line from Herman Melville's classic, *Moby Dick*. Recall the book's opening line: "Call me Ishmael." Clearly the opening line is Ishmael telling us his name. But if one places a comma after 'me', the result is the very different statement: "Call me, Ishmael." Now the sentence reads quite differently from Melville's original. Courtesy of the comma, someone is telling Ishmael to call him/her. Can you think of any other examples? If you can, please feel free to share them with me.

Exercises

I. Identify the component sentences in each compound sentence below.

1. David achieved his personal best but Sally did not.

2. Either Sue or Jill won but Jerry did not win.

3. Since it was late in the day, I didn't go to class.

4. If there's a test tomorrow then I need to study and get a good night's sleep.

5. I drink wine whenever I'm on a picnic.

6. Before she goes to school today, I want to tell Lorraine that I'm flying to Mexico today.

7. Even though it's Saturday, I went to the library to study.

II. Asserted or not? For each sentence below, identify its component sentences and say which of them are asserted and which not.

1. The vice president could be a big boost to Libby's defense but he may damage his reputation.

2. Science fiction gurus believe that Uncle Hugo's is the nation's oldest surviving sci-fi book store.

3. Napoleon, who recognized the danger to his right flank, personally led his troops against the enemy's position.

4. Newspaper columnist Robert Novak, whose disclosure of Plame's name kicked off the furor, said that Karl Rove told him about Plame's CIA connection.

5. St. Peter worked to get things back to normal after the tornado.

6. College professors, who make more money than they should, ought not insist that the academic calendar be shorterned.

7. Before the president left for the summit, his press secretary said that the president was excited but wary.

8. Judge Ito, the presiding judge, did not have adequate control of the court even though he believed that he had things under control.

9. The commissioner remarked that supervisors have to feel comfortable before drivers are sent out on the road.

10. At a crucial point in his life, Descartes dreamt that he discovered the foundation of all knowledge.

11. Confucius acknowledged that the divine right of kings was a central Chinese concept.

12. Platonists think mathematical entities can't be created but formalists know that mathematics is created by people.

13. If no medical problems pop up then Sam's doctor knows that the operation can proceed safely.

14. If no one knows the trouble I've seen then either everyone is blind or I'm invisible.

15. My swing coach, who is very sharp, has spotted several flaws in my swing.

16. Whether lawyers are honest is irrelevant to my argument.

17. Wise men say only fools fall in love but Jones believes love is good for the intellect.

18. Either Warner choked and Martz didn't have a good game plan or the Patriots are a great team.

19. Before Scrooge left for the day, he said that the Christmas bonus checks are in the mail.

20. No one is wiser than Socrates although everyone knows that he is a very odd man indeed.

21. It is a truth universally acknowledged that a rich single woman has absolutely no need for a husband. (Judith Ziemke)

22. Call me, Ishmael, but not before 9 am.

23. If you're going to get to heaven then you've got to raise a little hell.

When Statements Conflict: Contrary and Contradictory

Like countries and people, some statements conflict with others. When statements conflict, it means that they cannot both be true at the same time. If I say that Bob is presently playing golf and you say that Bob is presently in his study reading *Tropic of Cancer*, we have said conflicting things about Bob's present activities. That is, we cannot both be correct about Bob's present activities. I want to introduce an important distinction that can be made between statements that conflict with each other, that is, statements that cannot be simultaneously true. That distinction is between *contrary* propositions and *contradictory* propositions. We will meet this distinction again in a more formal guise in the chapter on categorical logic but it is best to get acquainted with its less formal cases, where it tends to be found in day-to-day language.

As for its importance to logic and philosophy, this distinction helps us recognize the difference between disagreements where one party is right and one wrong from disagreements where both parties cannot both be right but both may very well be wrong.

Exercises

I. For each pair of sentences, determine whether they are contraries, contradictories or not in conflict?

1. No students are rich.
2. It's not the case that all students are rich.

1. In 1996, the Army held its annual maneuvers in Spain.
2. The Army always holds its annual maneuvers in the United States.

1. The average salary for postal employees is no more than $48,000.
2. All postal employees make more than $50,000.

1. All employees must retire by age 70.
2. Some employees can retire at age 65.

1. No one called me all day (May 29).
2. Someone called me just before midnight (May 29).

1. It's false that some golfers are cheaters.
2. No golfers are cheaters.

1. Bob worked out two days last week, Tuesday and Thursday.
2. Bob did not work out on Thursday last week.

1. No one saw the president go into the White House at midnight.
2. Someone saw the president go into the White House at midnight.

1. The first person kicked off the island was Jeremy.
2. No, Jeremy was the second person kicked off the island.

1. The first rider of the night was Jess.
2. Jess was not the first rider of the night.

1. It's false that some spiders are not carnivorous.
2. No spiders are carnivorous.

1. It snowed for three solid hours yesterday.
2. We had no snow at all yesterday, nor any yet today.

1. It's false that some reporters are liberals.
2. All reporters are liberals.

1. Some students are not philosophy majors.
2. It's not the case that some students are philosophy majors.

1. No one saw O.J. do it.
2. Bill Gates saw O.J. do it.

1. Not all sailors are good swimmers.
2. Some sailors are good swimmers.

1. Bob is not married.
2. Bob is not single. (Assume Bob is an adult male person.)

1. The basketball was completely brown.
2. The basketball was both brown and blue.

1. The Wolves must score at least two more points to win.
2. The Wolves can win without scoring any more points.

1. Bob saw it and Joe did not.
2. Bob did not see it.

1. The second person on the moon was Buzz Aldrin.
2. There has been only one person on the moon.

1. Bob is older than Joe.
2. Joe is not younger than Bob.

1. Bob is older than Joe.
2. Joe is older than Bob.

1. Some people are unmarried.
2. No people are unmarried.

1. Some people are unflappable.
2. All people are flappable.

1. Neither a plane nor a train are quick enough for me.
2. Either a plane or a train is quick enough for me.

1. Tom is not both a student and a professor.
2. Tom is a professor but not a student.

Implication

Another important relation between sentences, and one we saw a bit earlier in the introductory chapter, is that of *implication*. One statement 'p' implies another 'q' just in case anytime 'p' is true, 'q' must be true as well.

Exercises

I. For each pair of statements, determine if the first statement implies the second. Some of the examples may be debatable due to questions about how some of the terms are to be understood. If you encounter such cases, consider how the different meanings affect the relations between the statements.

1. Only friends of mine are invited to the party.
   All friends of mine are invited to the party.

2. Anyone who loves AC/DC loves Zeppelin.
   Anyone who doesn't love Zeppelin doesn't love AC/DC.

3. If you work hard, you'll be successful.
   If you don't work hard, you won't be successful.

4. Only soft spikes are permitted on the course.
   Soft spikes are permitted only on the course.

5. All dogs are animals.
   Some dogs are animals.

6. Some of my cats are fickle.
   Some of my cats are not fickle.

7. Everything has a cause.
   There is a cause for everything.

8. The grades won't be posted if I'm out of town.
   The grades will be posted if I'm not out of town.

9. The dancers are as graceful as they are talented.
   The dancers are graceful and talented.

10. The contest is open to anyone who is a student or a professor.
    The contest is open to anyone who is both a student and a professor.

Phil. 110: Logic and Critical Thinking Pretest 1

I. (5 points) Completion. Fill in the blank in each case.

1. If two propositions p and q are related so that they always have opposite truth values, they are called _____ propositions.

2. The _____ of a concept are concrete objects that taken as a whole comprise the extension of the concept

3. ANIMAL is a genus with respect to BIRD but a species with respect to _____ .

4. According to our rules for definitions, a good definition must not _____ .

5. The sentence: MSU students who live in the dorms have an average GPA of 3.0, contains a _____ clause.

II. (10 points). For each of the following concepts, provide three referents. Having done this, find another concept to which the three referents can be said to belong.

1. ACTOR

2. MOVIE

III. (8 points) Arrange only one of the following groups of terms in order of increasing abstractness.

1. integer, number, positive integer, prime number, rational number, real number

2. animal, canine, English terrier, mammal, vertebrate, herding dog

IV. (9 points) Identify the genus and differentia for one of the following definitions and then determine whether it violates rule 3. Provide counterexamples and say explicitly whether they show the definition to be too broad or too narrow.

1. painting: picture drawn on a canvas with a brush

2. raincoat: outer garment of rubber that doesn't absorb water

V. (10 points). Each of the following definitions fails to satisfy at least one of our six marks for goo definitions. Choose three of them and say which rule (except rule 3) each of the three breaks.

(i) SOBER: the condition of not being drunk

(ii) BELIEF: the demi-cadence which closes a musical phrase in the symphony of our intellectual life

(iii) MEANING: a property of a word contained in an explanation of its meaning

(iv) DOG: a furry animal used by people as a plaything

(v) ANALYSIS: the act of analyzing the contradictions in things

(vi) EATING: when you put things in your mouth and chew and swallow them

VI. (8 points). Provide a classification scheme for the following terms:

DOG, COLLIE, CARDINAL, BLUE JAY, COCKER SPANIEL, Rover, Tweety

VII. (8 points). For one of the following concepts, provide at least three different principles you might use to generate various species for the concept. (Don't give me the species, just the principles).

a. Dinnerware

b. Automobiles

VIII. (18 points). For each sentence identify the component propositions and then determine which of them are asserted and which are not.

1. If the weather stays lousy then I'm going to California and I'm not coming back.

2. Before Wittgenstein studied at Cambridge, he said that he visited Gottlob Frege and that Frege influenced him considerably.

3. Joe is convinced that Hitchcock directed *Casablanca* but Larry is aware that it was directed by John Huston.

IX. (15 points). For each of the following pairs of sentences determine whether they are contraries, contradictories, or neither.

1. (a) No borogoves are mimsy.

    (b) Some borogoves are mimsy.

2. (a) Joe's dog Spot is a purebred terrier.

    (b) Joe's dog Spot is not a purebred at all.

3. (a) Oscar Mayer hot dogs are less than 40% pork.

    (b) Oscar Mayer hot dogs are more than 40% pork.

4. (a) Every person has a beetle.

    (b) Bob is a person and doesn't have a beetle.

5. (a) It's false that some students are not attending.

   (b) It's false that some students are attending.

X. (9 points). For each pair of propositions, decide whether the first proposition implies or entails the second proposition.

1. (i) Dogs are as lovable as they are intelligent. (ii) Dogs are lovable and intelligent.

2. (i) Einstein is a genius. (ii) Einstein is a genius or Einstein is a charlatan.

3. (i) If you don't read the book, you won't pass the test. (ii) If you read the book, you'll pass the test.

Chapter 5: Arguments – A Less Formal Story

To be clear-headed rather than confused; lucid rather than obscure; rational rather than otherwise; and to be neither more, nor less, sure of things than is justifiable by argument or evidence. That is worth trying for.   Philosopher Geoffrey Warnock

The mark of a logical proposition is *not* general [truth]. To be general means no more than to be accidentally [true] for all things.   Ludwig Wittgenstein

Fussy definition of 'argument': Two or more declarative sentences/statements, one or more of which (the premises) is alleged to provide reasons to believe, (or support for), one of the sentences/statements (the conclusion). (This fussy definition contrasts with the unfussy one from chapter 1, where I distinguished between arguments and immediate inferences. We'll use the fussy definition for the remainder of the book).

Logicians use the term 'argument' for a set of sentences whose job it is to convince someone of the truth of one of those sentences. As we already know, an argument can do this by being either deductive or inductive in character. For the first part of this chapter however, I will not be concerned about whether the arguments we look at are best understood to be deductive or inductive, truth functional, fallacious, valid, scientific, quantificational, etc. I simply want to focus on what arguments are and to get clear on the relation between premises and conclusions in arguments.

It is usual for logic texts to distinguish arguments from sets of sentences that are not arguments. So a set of sentences that describes some state of affairs in some detail, for example,

The U.S. auto industry is gasping under the crushing weight of high labor costs, growing competition and bloated, aging infrastructure. At the same time, the United Auto Workers union is struggling to stay relevant after years of membership declines. Caught between them in this years contract talks are the workers who built middle-class lives on the promises of the industry,

is simply a set of related sentences describing the current situation in the auto industry and related issues concerning its workers. No one would be tempted to regard this set of sentences as an argument, and for good reason. For there is no attempt to use one or more of these statements as support for one of the other statements.

But now consider the following:

Doctor to Bob's family after Bob was taken to the hospital after falling down a flight of stairs: "Bob fell down the steps because he was suffering from low blood sugar."

As we know from the previous chapter, the doctor's statement is best seen as two statements connected together by 'because'. And here it might be thought that the doctor is offering an argument for the truth of the first statement, 'Bob fell down the steps' on the basis of the second statement, 'Bob was suffering from low blood sugar'. While it is true that 'because' is often used in the course of giving arguments, I would suggest that the doctor is not offering an argument but rather is explaining why something happened, namely, why Bob fell down the steps. That Bob fell down the steps is probably something the family already knows to be true and so is not something they need to have established as true. On the other hand, consider:

Bob is coming to the reunion because he knows Marlene will be there.

In this case, the 'because' statement can quite plausibly be read as offering us an argument for the conclusion, 'Bob is coming to the party'. To be sure, this statement could have been uttered by someone trying to explain something already known to be true, namely, that Bob was coming to the reunion. But it is also easy to imagine the statement made by someone who was trying to convince him/herself or others that Bob was in fact going to be at the reunion.

These cases bring out both the similarities and differences between arguments and explanations. In both explanations and arguments, we are being offered reasons for the truth of some statement or other. But the difference between arguments and explanations is that in an argument, the statement for which we are offered reasons for its truth is one which we are not yet fully convinced is true. In the case of an explanation, on the other hand, the statement for which we are being offered reasons is one that we already know to be true, albeit without being sure about how or why it came to be true. Although I will not be further concerned with distinguishing arguments from explanations, it is worth appreciating that most explanations can be regarded as a kind of incomplete argument, namely, one whose premise is the stated explanation, X occurred because Y did, and whose conclusion is the causal statement, X caused Y. That said, from here on to the end of the chapter, our focus shall be arguments because that's where the fun is.

How one comes to appreciate that some set of sentences is in fact an argument is largely a function of contextual clues, experience, and, for lack of a better term, argument language, better known as premise and conclusion indicating language. The terms in the box below are common premise and conclusion indicators of English. Don't try to learn the entire list but it would be a good idea to learn the first three or four terms of each list, as they are used more regularly than the others.

Premise Indicators	Conclusion Indicators
since	therefore
because	hence
for/for one thing	thus/ergo
for the reason that	so
follows from	follows that
inasmuch as	consequently
as shown by	which entails that
given that	which proves that
seeing that	which implies that
owing to	necessarily
seeing that	must be the case that
as/as indicated by	which means that
assuming that	demonstrates that
considering that	we can conclude that
	as a result

As we already know in the case of 'because', many of the words in the box are not used exclusively to mark premises and conclusions in arguments. So the presence of such terms among sentences does not guarantee that an argument is afoot. It is also possible that you may encounter an argument that contains no premise or conclusion indicating terms. Still, when an argument does contain some of the terms in the table above, it will make the analysis of arguments much easier by far.

Diagramming Arguments

It will prove both useful and somewhat interesting to learn how to diagram an argument in a way that will make clear how its premises and conclusion(s) hang together. A simple and popular diagramming technique is that we will use is due to the philosopher Monroe Beardsley.

Exercises

I. Provide a Beardsley diagram for each of the following arguments.

1. The Wolves have been on a losing streak lately. Now the Wolves' losing streak is due to the Boston trade or to Casey's recent juggling of the lineup. But Casey juggled the lineup earlier in the year with some success. It's clear then that the Wolves' losing streak is due to the Boston trade.

2. If an action promotes the best interests of everyone concerned and violates no one's rights, then that action is morally acceptable. In at least some cases, active euthanasia promotes the best interests of everyone concerned and violates no one's rights. Thus, in at least some cases, active euthanasia is morally acceptable.

3. Because of a narrowing definition of who was a true conservative, a great tightening has occurred in the Republican Party. Apostates and deviationists were expelled and party leaders sought purity above all. As a result, the conservative movement is in something of a decline.

4. Neah Bay, the northwestern-most city in the continental United States, lies on the shore of an arm of the Pacific Ocean. This means not only that it enjoys Mediterranean-like weather throughout the year, but also that it has significant amounts of rain during the winter.

5. The truth is that politics and money are inseparable, and as money has greed as its foundation, necessarily, greed and politics are connected.

6. We should not adopt a policy of socialized medicine because it would result in the deterioration of the quality of medical care and it could bankrupt the federal government. This isn't rocket science people.

7. Nothing is demonstrable unless the contrary implies a contradiction. Nothing that is . . . conceivable implies a contradiction. Whatever we conceive as existent, we can also conceive as nonexistent. There is no being, therefore, whose non-existence implies a contradiction. Consequently, there is no being whose existence is demonstrable. (David Hume).

8. Natural selection builds child brains with a tendency to believe whatever their parents tell them. Such trusting obedience is valuable for survival. But the flip side of trusting obedience is slavish gullibility. Thus, children typically adopt and accept the religion of their parents.

9. Because of the radicalization of American universities in the 1960s, many academics regarded those who disagreed with them as non-intellectual dupes, and many non-intellectuals dismissed academia as hotbed of leftist propaganda. Thus, the connection between academia (and especially philosophy) and the public was sundered and remains so to the present day.

10. People cannot avoid their fate. If no one can avoid his/her fate then any action is pointless; what will be will be. Thus, sitting in a robe and uttering "OM" all day is as good as any other action.

11. The new marketing campaign highlighting the livability of the Twin Cities is all wrong. We shouldn't be trying to attract people, we should be trying to repel people. Thus, our new marketing slogan should be: "Minneapolis-St. Paul: A Cold Omaha."

Preserving the Truth

Now that we know how to identify and diagram arguments, it is time to turn to a consideration of an argument's most important property, namely, its ability, or lack thereof, to preserve the truth. An argument can be good only if its premises, when true, make a good case for the truth of its conclusion. We know that deductively valid arguments provide a guarantee of the truth of their conclusions anytime their premises are true, and who can ask for more than that? We also know that inductively strong arguments are such that it's a good bet that the conclusion is true whenever its premises are true. It is now time to get a bit more specific about how to tell deductively valid arguments from invalid ones.

Valid truth-functional argument forms:

Disjunctive syllogism: p or q, not p, therefore, q

Modus ponens: If p then q, p, therefore, q

Modus tollens: If p then q, not q, therefore, not p

Hypothetical argument: If p then q, if q then r, therefore, If p then r

Constructive dilemma: Either p or q, if p then r, if q then s, therefore, either r or s.

If and only if argument: p if and only if q, q, therefore p

Invalid truth-functional forms:

p or q, p, therefore not q

Denying the antecedent: If p then q, not p, therefore not q

Affirming the consequent: If p then q, q, therefore p

Some common English expressions and their truth functional equivalents:

p only if q = If p then q (another equivalent is: If not q then not p)

p if q = If q then p

p unless q = p or q (Also: If not q then p, as well as: If not p then q)

p given that q = If q then p

Assuming that p, q = If p then q

Neither p nor q = Not (p or q) (Also, Not p and not q)

Not both p and q = Not (p and q) (Also: Not p or not q)

Exercises

I. Decide for each argument whether it is valid or invalid

1. p unless q, not p, thus, q

2. p if q, not q, thus, not p

3. p or q, q, thus, p

4. If p then q, q, thus, p

5. p only if q, not p, thus, not q

6. not (p and q), not p, thus, q

7. p if and only if q, q, thus p

8. p or q, p, thus, not q

9. p given that q, p, thus, q

10. Neither p nor q, thus, not p

11. p only if not q, q, thus, not p.

12. not p unless q, not q, thus, p.

13. If p then q, If p then r, thus, if q then r.

14. p unless not q, p, thus, q.

II. For each argument below, put it into standard truth-functional form and then determine whether the resulting argument is valid. In the first two exercises, use the suggested letters to represent propositions. In the remaining cases, feel free to create your own letters to represent propositions.

1. George must be a big believer in vitamins. He bought over $100 worth of vitamins yesterday, and he would do that only if he believed in vitamins. (G, V)

2. Anarchy would work if men were angels. Alas, they are not. So anarchy won't work. (A, M)

3. If the cardinals show up, the feeder is not empty. The cardinals showed up. Thus, the feeder is not empty.

4. Bob will show up unless he is ill. There is Bob now. He must not be ill.

5. The paper turns red if it's dipped in beer. It turned red. Thus, it was dipped in beer.

6. Eastwood won't win unless Scorcese loses. But Scorcese will lose. So Eastwood will win.

7. Oswald killed Kennedy only if Fetzer's ideas are nutty. But Fetzer's ideas are nutty. Thus, Oswald killed Kennedy.

Three Kinds of Truth-Functional Statements
Individual statements of truth-functional logic can be put into three different categories, as follows:

1. **Tautologies** -- always true, true under all possible assignments of truth-values to atomic statements.
2. **Self-contradictory** -- always false, false under all possible assignments of truth-values to atomic statements.
3. **Contingent** -- true on at least one assignment of truth-values to its component statements, and false on at least one assignment of truth-values to its component statements.

First Logic

Exercises

I. Determine whether the following are tautologies, self-contradictory or contingent.

1. If p then p
2. If p then not p
3. (p and not q) or not p
4. (p and not q) or (not p or q)
5. (If not p then (p and q)) and not p
6. If p then (q and not p)
7. Not (if (p and not p) then (q or s))
8. (p and not p) if and only if (q and not q)
9. If (p or q) then p
10. If q then (r and not r)
11. If (p and q) then (p or q)
12. If not p then (p or not q)

Another important relation in truth-functional land is that of *implication*: One compound statement implies another just in case there is no row of the truth table in which the first statement is true and the second one is false.

Exercises

I. Decide whether the first statement implies the second.

1. p; If q then p
2. If q then p; p
3. p or not p; q
4. p and not p; q
5. p; p or q
6. p and not q; not q

Finally, when two truth-functional statements imply each other, they are *logically equivalent*. More formally, we'll say that two compound statements are logically equivalent just in case they have the same truth-values in every case (or have the same truth table).

Exercises

I. Determine for each pair of statements whether they are logically equivalent.

1. If p then q; not p or q
2. p and (p or q); p
3. If q then not q; if p then not p
4. If p then p; If q then q
5. If p then (If q then p); If p then p
6. p if and only if q; (p and q) or (not p and not q)
7. If not p then (q and r); p or (r and q)
8. If (p and q) then (p or q) ; If p then p
9. If p then q; if not q then not p
10. p if and only if not p; (p and q) and (r and not p)

Chapter 6: Informal Fallacies

I have been in love with logic ever since my father started me on logic in my teens. Logic of itself cannot give anyone the answer to any questions of substance; but without logic we often do not know the import of what we know and often fall into fallacy and inconsistency.
Peter Geach, philosopher

If the world were a logical place, men would ride side saddle.   Rita Mae Brown

As the notion is used and understood in introductory logic courses and texts, 'fallacy' means simply any bad argument. The term can be, and is, used in other ways too. In particular, it is often used to mean any false belief. For us, 'fallacy' will be used, as it has been traditionally used in logic, to refer to bad arguments. Although there are a number of fairly standard distinctions and classifications of fallacies in logic texts, it should be noted that a final and definitive list of fallacies is simply not possible. This is because there is no final list of the ways that reasoning can go badly or be misused by the unscrupulous.

Most texts divide fallacies into various categories, including categories like fallacies of ambiguity, of presumption, of relevance, formal, informal, etc. I too have my preferred way of classifying fallacies but I will not require that you learn my scheme and which fallacies I put into which category. The categories may serve as handy guides but I think the best way to learn fallacies is simply one by one, or more correctly, type by type. After you have learned the different types of fallacies, you can then devise your own classification scheme and compare it to my own.

List of Fallacies
Appeal to Majority: using the fact that a sizable number of people (or other entities, including countries or groups or organizations, etc.) believe, accept or want a statement to be true as a basis for concluding that the statement is true.
Appeal to Force: (argumentum ad baculum): trying to get someone to accept a statement, position, course of action, etc., by threatening his/her safety, finances, social standing, etc.
Appeal to (Unreliable) Authority (*argumentum ad verecundiam*): using the fact that an unreliable authority accepts or advocates a proposition as a basis for concluding that the proposition is true.
Ad hominem **(argument against the person)**: citing traits, facts or properties of a speaker as a basis for rejecting his/her argument or statements
    abusive AH (name calling): using terms of derision against a speaker;
    tu quoque: attempting to justify rejecting another's advice, criticism, recommendation, etc., by citing the fact that the person who gave the advice etc., doesn't adhere to it; (in short, the arguer accuses another of being a hypocrite).

First Logic

circumstantial AH: attempting to undermine another's argument or claim by citing facts about him/her that suggest, but do not establish, that the person's argument or claim is to be rejected.

False Alternative (Black and white thinking): An argument that relies on alternatives that seem to be exhaustive but are not; typically involves an either-or statement that makes use of contrary terms that seem to be contradictory terms; e.g., black/white, smart/stupid, friend/enemy, hot/cold, etc.

Hasty Generalization: drawing a general conclusion based on insufficient evidence, usually one or two instances are cited when many more are needed to properly support the general claim.

Appeal to Ignorance (*argumentum ad ignorantiam*): using a premise (or premises) that there is no proof or evidence against (for) a particular statement as a basis for concluding that the statement is true (false).

Post Hoc (*post hoc ergo propter hoc*): citing the fact that one event (E) happened after another (C) as a basis for concluding that the prior event (C) caused the latter (E); trying to justify a causal claim by appeal simply to the fact that the alleged cause occurred before the alleged effect.

Diversion/Red Herring: arguing for a conclusion that is not really at issue and which in fact is not relevant to the questions or issues being discussed.

Straw Man: arguing or responding to another person's claim or argument by distorting it so as to make it easily refutable or easy to reject.

Begging the Question/Circular Argument: trying to argue for a statement by using that statement (or something that is effectively identical to it) as a premise, or by presupposing the truth of that statement in another argument. Other forms of this fallacy include **complex question**, which involves asking someone a question which presupposes the truth of something that has yet to be established; e.g., "Have you stopped beating your wife yet?", and **question-begging definition**, which involves defining a term so as to make a statement in question true.

Division: this fallacy is committed when one illegitimately supposes that what is true (or false) of a whole is true (or false) of its parts as well (or what is true or false of a group is true or false of its members).

Composition: This is the reverse of DIVISION. This fallacy is committed when one illegitimately supposes that what is true (or false) of the parts of a whole is also true (or false) of the whole composed out of those parts (or what is true or false of the members of the group is true or false of the group as whole).

Equivocation: This fallacy results from an illegitimate shift of meaning in an argument. Usually, a single term or short phrase is used in two different senses in the course of the argument.

Amphiboly: This fallacy results from faulty or problematic formal structure in a statement. The faulty structure leads to misinterpretation, which in turn leads to unlikely and implausible conclusions being drawn. Newspaper headlines and advertisements are a wonderful source of amphiboly.

"TO BE" fallacy: In this fallacy, one confuses the "is" of identity with the "is" of predication. The "is" of identity occurs most often in mathematical contexts, e.g.,

68

"2 X 3 is 6". But when we say: "The sky is blue", we are not saying that the sky is identical with the color blue but rather we are predicating the property blue to the sky. When these two senses of "is" are confused, the result is ambiguity and fallacy.

Exercises

I. Identify any fallacies you find in the following examples.

1. There can't be laws without a lawmaker, a being who makes the laws. But nature, as science itself makes clear, operates according to strict laws, like the law of gravity and the law of conservation of energy. So there must be a lawmaker above nature, namely God.

2. Criminal actions are illegal, and all murder trials are criminal actions, thus all murder trials are illegal.
(Example borrowed from I. Copi.)

3. The sign said "fine for parking here", and since it was fine, I parked there.

4. Sodium and chlorine, the basic components of salt, are both deadly poisons. Thus, salt must be a deadly poison.

5. According to Euclid's geometry, a plane is a two-dimensional surface that is perfectly flat. The F-15 is a plane, hence the F-15 is a two-dimensional surface

6. Conventional bombs did more damage in W.W. II than nuclear bombs. Thus, a conventional bomb is more dangerous than a nuclear bomb. (From I. Copi).

7. Because the brain, which is made up entirely of neural cells, is capable of consciousness, it follows that each neural cell in the brain must be capable of consciousness.

8. Iraq is a militant and violent country. Thus, Iraqi citizens are militant and violent people.

9. The newspaper headline said, "Police vow to stop illegal gambling in River City." I'm glad to see that the police are finally cleaning up their act.

10. Nothing is better than God. A hot dog is better than nothing. Thus, a hot dog is better than God.

11. Mystic to Hot Dog Vendor: Make me one with everything.

12. Maria is the shortest player on the volleyball team. All the members of the volleyball team are women. Thus, Maria is a short woman.

13. A car consumes less fuel than an airplane. Thus, less fuel is consumed by cars in the United States than by airplanes.

14. Every sentence in this paragraph is well written. Thus, the paragraph is well written.

15. Nadal and Federer are the two best tennis players on the planet. Clearly, they would make the best tennis doubles team on the planet.

16. The U.S. Congress is incompetent and ineffective. Therefore, Congressman Gephardt must incompetent and ineffective.

17. Bill said he was interviewing for a job flying fighter jets in the Air Force recruiter's office. Wow, who knew that the Air Force gave its recruiters such big offices.

18. All humans are mortal. Therefore, at some point, no humans will exist anywhere in the universe.

19. A few minutes after the priest finished his sermon, a lightning bolt struck the steeple. Obviously, God didn't like what the priest had to say today.

20. There are more casinos in Las Vegas than in any other city in the nation, and yet it has less violent crime per capita than any city in the country. The facts are clear: If we want to reduce violent crime, we must build more casinos.

21. The best case I know to show that the tax cut bill will not hurt the middle class by reducing funding for governmental services is the fact that Senator Edwards, a vigilant watchdog for the middle class, gave the bill his unqualified recommendation.

22. On a recent date, I swear the guy I was out with had at least six arms, if you know what I mean. Last week, another date of mine insisted that the best way for a woman to get to know a man was to have sex with him. Let's face it, all men think about is sex.

23. Evangelist Jimmy Swaggert claims that sex education classes in our public schools are promoting promiscuity among the young. That's good enough for me: We should abolish such classes.

24. Eight out of ten doctors support a woman's right to have an abortion. How can anyone deny that this is a genuine right?

25. A recent column in the *Star Tribune* expressed sympathy for atheism, suggesting that belief in God could not be rationally justified. I think I'm going to have to cancel my subscription now that the *Strib* has stooped to advocating satanism.

26. William Buckley has argued in favor of legalizing drugs such as marijuana, cocaine and heroin. But Buckley is just another of those upper-crust intellectuals who is out of touch with America. Thus, we should reject his claim that drugs should be legal.

27. Professor Rorty has argued on many occasions that truth is not the most important thing in life. Apparently, he advocates error, falsehoods and lying. And the dangers of mistakes and lying are clear and obvious to everyone. Let's then reject Rorty's advocacy of lies and errors.

28. Politicians should stop asking voters what they want from their representatives. After all, most people want to have their lives made easier and so will ask their representatives to legislate handouts and pork for them and their friends and family.

29. Neoatheists like Richard Dawkins and Sam Harris have argued that belief in God is without any scientific or rational foundation. But people have always believed in God and many people couldn't face their daily life without believing in God and his goodness.

30. Members of the mainstream media who criticize Fox News are not worth taking seriously. After all, they're nothing but a bunch of liberals and no claims by liberals are worth taking seriously.

31. My daughter was told by her Sunday School teacher that God made no one else like her. My gosh, what a cruel thing to say to a child. Even if it were true, telling a child that could undermine her faith in God.

Phil. 110: Intro to Logic & Critical Thinking Pretest 2

I. (10 points). Fill in the blank with the appropriate term or short phrase.

1. An argument that is missing either a premise or a conclusion is an
_____ .

2. In a standard form conditional statement, the first statement is called the
_____ and the second statement is called the _____ .

3. A truth-functional statement that is true on all truth-value assignments to its
component statements is a _____ .

4. The fallacy of _____ occurs when a word is given two
meanings (i.e., expresses two different concepts) in the course of an argument.

5. One form of the fallacy of ad hominem is _____ .

II. (15 points). Give a Beardsley diagram for each of the following arguments. (Be
sure to make clear what statements your numbers refer to.)

1. Someone robbed the bank at midnight. Now the robbery was an inside job or it
was done by a professional. But the bank employees are too honest to be part of
an inside job. Thus, the bank robbery had to be carried out by a professional.

2. The Tao cannot exist. For if Tao exists, it is either present or absent. But Tao
cannot be absent since the absent cannot govern actions. But it's also the case that
Tao cannot be present, since the present is subject to change and perishing. Thus,
Tao cannot exist.

3. The influence of religion on our culture has resulted in irrational laws
concerning recreational drugs. Anyone who believes that God is up in heaven and
unhappy with those who do drugs, will believe that drug use is wrong and ought to
be punished. Thus, the religious advocate punishment for those who do drugs.
But punishment for recreational drug use is about as rational as punishing those
who drink beer or coffee or who smoke cigarettes.

III. (15 points). For each of the following arguments, identify the premise and conclusion and then provide the implicit/assumed premise.

1. Since teenagers drink more caffeine than their parents, it follows that teenagers have more trouble getting to sleep at night.

2. Because anyone who seeks enjoyment at the expense of others is heartless and exploitive, the producers of reality TV shows are heartless and exploitive.

3. Consciousness cannot be explained by the laws of physics so, it is not a physical phenomenon.

IV. (25 points). For each of the following arguments, determine whether the argument form is valid. If it is not valid, provide a set of truth-values for its component statements that show this.

1. not p only if q
   not p
   not p

2. q unless p
   not p
   q

3. p if q
   p
   q

4. p unless not q
   q
   p

5. p only if q
   p if r
   q if r

V. (15 points). Determine for each of the following whether it is a tautology, contradiction or contingent. If it is contingent, provide a set of truth-values for p, q, r, that make it true, as well as a set of truth-values for p, q, r, that make it false.

1. If p then (q and not q)

2. (p or not p) and q

3. Not (q and r) or (If r then not q)

VI. (20 points). Identify the fallacies in the following passages.

1. Going to golf college is no way to get ahead in the golf world since spending time in college classrooms and on college campuses will not help one make money in golf.

2. The campus committee has recently come out in favor of allowing bingo games for fundraising on campus. But such an idea is lame and should be rejected. How could anyone be in favor of the idea of allowing students to spend their entire day gambling? We'll probably have to cover the campus with casinos before too long in order to accommodate townies. Surely we have better things to do with the state's money than cover our campus with casinos.

3. People either have a natural talent for logic, or they are completely unable to do it, no matter what. Those with natural talent obviously have no need of instruction. Equally obvious though is that those completely unable to do logic will not gain from instruction. Thus instruction in logic is a waste of time.

4. Bob's car wreck occurred just a few short weeks after the Tarot card reader put a curse on him. That's proof enough that the Tarot card reader's curse worked.

5. Jones can run the half mile in just over 2 minutes, the mile in just over 4 minutes, therefore Jones can run 20 miles in just over 80 minutes.

6. *The Free Press* says it is going to carry a series of stories about this year's tornado starting on Thursday. We should clear out our cellar and put our valuables down there as well so as to be prepared for the tornado on Thursday.

7. Al: Clarence Thomas did not sexually harass Anita Hill.

Bob: How do you know that?

Al: No one has proved that he did so.

8. Charlie's argument against raising taxes ought not be taken seriously. After all, he was a miserable failure as a businessman and his wife left him for a richer man.

9. Man is the only animal that speaks a language. No woman is a man. Thus, no woman speaks a language.

10. Bob is a member of one of the heaviest partying fraternities on campus, and so he must be one of the biggest partiers on campus.

Chapter 7: Categorical Logic – The Logic of Aristotle

Philosophy is an activity that uses reasoning and rigorous argument to promote human flourishing.
Epicurus

Men are apt to mistake the strength of their feeling for the strength of their argument. The heated mind resents the chill touch and relentless scrutiny of logic.   William Gladstone

Categorical logic, or, Aristotelian logic, is at once simple and complex. It is also the most ancient part of logic, having been codified by Aristotle in his *Organon* 350 years B.C.E or thereabout. As one of its names implies, it is a logic focused on categories, that is, sets of things. In chapter 1, we looked at general terms and singular terms and both terms can be regarded as picking out categories of things. As such, these terms play an important role in Aristotle's logic. But by far the most important parts of categorical logic are its key logical terms, 'All', 'Some', 'No', 'are', 'are not', and 'non'. Unlike the logical terms we saw in chapter 5, namely, 'and', 'or', 'if-then', the key logical terms of categorical logic do not connect together sentences or statements in a truth-functional way. Rather, the logical terms of categorical logic allow us to speak about classes or categories and their members, and to ascribe properties to them. It is also interesting to note that until the early part of the twentieth century, categorical logic was considered to be pretty much the whole of logic.

Categorical logic consists of four fairly straightforward statement forms and the relations between them, as well as arguments formed from them. The relationships are summarized in what has come to be known as *the square of opposition*. (BTW: If this expression is said with the proper intonation and accompanied by the right music, it can send shivers of glee down your spine. How's that for excitement)? The arguments formed from categorical statements are known as syllogisms. Given their long history, it is not surprising to find references to syllogisms mentioned quite often in the writings of the famous and educated throughout history. I won't go so far as to say that knowing nothing about syllogisms is a sure sign of an inadequate education, but it's not far from the truth. And so to ensure your place among the ranks of the properly educated, let's get started on categorical logic.

The four categorical statements are the result of different combinations of four properties. Those properties are universal, particular, affirmative, and negative. The first two properties are quantity properties, while the last two are quality properties. Combining one quantity and one quality per sentence yields the following statements.

Universal Affirmative -- All S are P

Universal Negative -- No S are P

Particular Affirmative -- Some S are P

Particular Negative -- Some S are not P

> Tradition has christened the first statement the A-statement, the second is the E-statement, the third is an I-statement and the last is known as the O-statement. At this point, we can say that categorical logic consists of the A, E, I, and O statements and their relations and use in arguments.

The 'S' and 'P' in each statement are abbreviated stand-ins for category terms. The first such term in a categorical statement is called the subject term (which explains why we typically use 'S' as a stand-in for it) and the second term in a categorical statement is called the predicate term (hence the use of 'P' to represent it). As noted above, any general term or singular term can be a term in a categorical statement, although the singular terms take a little bit of massaging to get them to be categorical terms in good standing. Finally, the 'are' and 'are not' are called the copula of the statement. "Copula' is just a term borrowed from the Greeks that means "connection". The copula connects the subject term with the predicate term.

But beyond the terms of chapter 1, a little bit of work can turn adjectives and verb phrases into category terms. As a result of this, many sentences of English that do not at all resemble categorical sentences can nonetheless be made to fit quite easily into Aristotle's A, E, I, O forms. For example, consider the statement, No golfers cheat. As it stands, it is not quite a standard form categorical statement, for two reasons. One, it does not have a copula and, two, the word 'cheat' is a verb rather than a term that picks out a category. But English has a variety of ways of going from a verb to a category term. In this case, the simplest maneuver is to add 'ers' to get 'cheaters', a category term in good standing. Add a copula and we get the E-statement: No golfers are cheaters, or more simply, No G are C. Another maneuver would have been to talk of "people who cheat", and take that to be our predicate term, yielding the equivalent E-statement, No golfers are people who cheat, or more simply, No G are P.

Consider now a slightly messier example: Some vintage autos are wildly overpriced. Although we have a compound subject term, we can still treat it as a subject term, 'V', say, for vintage autos. 'Wildly overpriced', however, needs some work. The easiest thing to do here is to add an innocuous class term to it, that is, something like 'things' or 'objects', to get our predicate term. Thus, we get the I-statement, Some vintage autos are wildly overpriced things, or more simply, Some V are W.

I mentioned above that singular terms can be turned into category terms, and the process is as follows. Consider the sentence, Socrates is mortal. Although it is most tempting to treat this as an I statement (after all, it certainly doesn't seem to be universal), and even though there is nothing logically wrong about doing so, tradition has it that singular term statements, that is, statements whose subject term is singular, are treated as universal statements (A or E, depending on the content of the sentence in question). We turn 'Socrates' into the singleton class term, 'S' for 'things identical to Socrates', 'mortal' becomes 'M', for 'mortal things', and the English becomes the categorical, All S are M. If we had a negative statement about Socrates, say, Socrates was not a kind-hearted fellow, we would get the E-statement, 'No S are K', where 'S' again stands for 'things identical to Socrates' and 'K' stands for 'kind-hearted fellows'.

Other things to keep in mind when going from English to categorical statements:

1. Unlike categorical sentences, subjects do not always appear first in English sentences, nor predicates second. Be especially careful about this when translating A and O categorical statements.

2. English has a variety of less than specific quantity terms, as well as terms that sometimes behave as universals, and other times behave as particular quantity terms.

3. 'All S are not P' is not a categorical statement.

Distribution of Terms
A very important, but not exactly perspicuous, property of categorical sentences is that of distribution. I recommend that students simply learn or commit to memory which terms are distributed in which categorical statements. It will serve you well when you are asked to evaluate categorical syllogisms for validity. The distribution facts are as follows:

The A statement distributes the subject term only

The E statement distributes both the subject term and predicate term

The I statement distributes no terms (neither the subject nor predicate)

The O statement distributes the predicate term only

Exercises

I. Translate each of the following sentences into a standard form categorical statement and say which terms are distributed in each case.

1. A watched pot never boils.

2. Never give a sucker an even break. (No suckers are persons you should give an even break.)

3. Some golfers cheat.

4. Anyone who likes movies enjoys the Academy Awards.

5. A rose smells sweet.

6. Europe is a small continent.

7. All French citizens are not opposed to the war.

8. A few textbooks for the course are expensive.

9. A few textbooks for the course are not expensive.

10. Every good boy deserves favor.

11. Snakes are not cuddly creatures.

12. George Washington was not always honest.

13. There are three of the enemy yet to be exterminated.

14. Anyone who wants to can request a transcript.

15. Whenever it snows, I have to shovel the walk.

16. Only humans pray.

17. A mind is a terrible thing to waste.

18. I'm not happy today.

19. Bob is due in at noon.

20. If a stick moves, it's a snake.

21. JFK was not a friend of mine.

22. There are a couple of beers in the fridge.

23. Bob always takes his lucky rabbit's foot to work.

24. Sue never brings her lunch to school.

25. Nobody's perfect.

Categorical Operations

There are three well-known operations that one can perform on categorical statements. They are *conversion*, *obversion* and *contraposition*. Each of these operations changes a categorical statement in one way or another, either switching its terms, changing its quality, or altering its terms. Our main interest in these operations will concern the logical relations, if any, between categorical statements and the statements that result from performing the operations on them. More specifically, we will be interested in which operations yield logically equivalent statements on which categorical statements.

Exercises

I. How are the following pairs of statements logically related (i.e., converse, obverse, contrapositive, contrary, contradictory, subaltern, subcontrary)?

1. No squirrel is an island. Some squirrels are not islands.

2. Some books are not fit for teens. Some books are unfit for teens.

3. All students are scholars. All scholars are students.

4. No cars are reliable. All cars are unreliable.

5. Some cases of fraud are hard to prove. Some cases of fraud are not hard to prove.

6. No disreputable people can be happy. No unhappy people are reputable.

7. All college expenses are tax-deductible. Some tax-deductible items are college expenses.

8. Some chemicals are not toxic. Some nontoxic things are not nonchemicals.

9. Some golfers are not happy about the course setup. Some who are happy about the course setup were not golfers.

10. There are no stupid questions. There are some stupid questions.

11. Everyone likes to eat hot foods. Some don't like to eat hot foods.

12. All animals are equal. Some animals are more equal than others.

II. For each of the following, "Make the move" or determine that it cannot be made.

1. All T are H. Some T are not non-H.
2. No G are P. All P are non-G.
3. All H are B. Some B are H.
4. Some S are non-L. Some non-L are not non-S.
5. All F are N. All N are non-F.
6. No I are S. Some S are non-I.
7. All G are non-H. Some non-G are H.
8. No non-D are C. Some C are not D.
9. Some persons are litterbugs. Some litterbugs are not non-persons.
10. All quacks are non-doctors. All doctors are non-quacks.
11. No Americans are Buddhists. Some Americans are non-Buddhists.
12. No contemporary texts are philosophical texts. Some philosophical texts are not contemporary texts.
13. No students are infants. All infants are non-students.
14. All durable items are taxable. Some non-taxable things are non-durable items.
15. All wrenches are metal. Some things that are not wrenches are things that are not metal.
16. No butterflies are moths. Some non-butterflies are moths.

Syllogisms

When you take exactly three different terms, call them 'S', 'P' and 'M' (for reasons which I hope will become obvious to you shortly), and use them twice each to form three categorical statements, and put them in a particular order, and make one the conclusion and the other two its premises, the result will be a *syllogism*. A syllogism's key characteristics, indeed, its defining characteristics, are known as mood and figure. Once you know a syllogism's mood and figure, you know everything you need to reconstruct it and to determine whether it is valid or not.

The mood of a syllogism is a function of the type of categorical statements that are the syllogism's first premise (also called the major premise), the second premise (also known as the minor premise) and finally its conclusion. For example, if the major premise is an A statement, the minor premise is an E statement and the conclusion is an O statement, the mood would be AEO. As for the figure, that is a function of the position of the middle term, the term that appears only in the syllogism's premises. A bit of reflection will allow you to see that there are four different positions that the middle term can have in a syllogism. In the first figure, the middle term is in subject place of the major premise and in the predicate spot in the minor premise. Reverse those positions and you get the fourth figure. In the second figure, the middle term is in the predicate spot in both premises while in the third figure, the middle term is in the subject position in both premises.

Exercises

I. Determine the mood and figure of each syllogism and then determine whether it is valid by our rules or Venn diagrams.

1. No Greek philosopher was a genius because geniuses are brilliant and no Greek philosophers were brilliant.

2. No machine is capable of perpetual motion because every machine is subject to friction and no such thing is capable of perpetual motion.

3. Some things that are worth buying are expensive, for Gucci suits are expensive and some of them are worth buying.

4. It's clear that Betty is a conservative. She voted for Bush in the last election and only conservatives voted for Bush.

5. Radical groups do not obey the laws of the U.S. government. Since polygamists do not accept the laws of the U.S. government, they must be a radical group.

6. Some cars that run on electricity are quite sporty. Thus, some sporty cars are not gas guzzlers, since no gas guzzlers run on electricity.

7. No man is an island. Man is a social animal. Thus, some social animals are not islands.

8. All great golfers are geniuses but none of them is imprudent. Thus, some geniuses are not imprudent.

9. Alton Brown is a Food Network star, thus, he won't be coming to my house anytime soon, for no Food Network stars are coming to my house in the near future.

10. *Moby Dick* is a great novel but since not all great novels make great movies, it's not surprising that *Moby Dick* isn't a great movie.

Enthymemes

In real life, whatever that is, people are not always as fussy about their syllogisms as logicians are. They often present what we would regard as an incomplete syllogism, leaving a premise or conclusion unstated, typically because they regard it as too obvious to be worth stating. Such incomplete syllogisms are called *enthymemes*. To take a typical example, someone might argue that Socrates must be mortal, given that he is a human being. Here the unstated premise is, All persons are mortal. A fun and useful exercise is to find a missing premise (or, in some cases, a missing conclusion) for an enthymeme that will yield a valid syllogism.

Exercises

I. Turn the following enthymemes into valid syllogisms by adding in the missing premise or conclusion and identify the resulting mood and figure as well.

1. Mechanistic materialists do not believe in free will because they think that everything is governed by deterministic laws.

2. All nonprofit organizations are exempt from paying taxes, so churches must be exempt.

3. Animals that are loved by someone should not be sold to a medical laboratory, and lost pets are certainly loved by someone.

4. Higher life forms could not have evolved through merely random processes, because no organized beings could have evolved that way.

5. It isn't true that all politicians are honest, for some have taken bribes.

II. By appeal to our rules for valid syllogisms, see if you can prove each of the following claims.

1. The conclusion of valid syllogism in the second figure must be negative (E or O).
2. A valid syllogism cannot have two particular premises.
3. In a valid syllogism of the third figure, the conclusion must be particular.
4. In a valid syllogism of the first figure, the minor premise must be affirmative.
5. A valid syllogism with a particular premise, must have a particular conclusion as well.

III. For each of the following syllogisms, determine mood and figure and then test it for validity.

All P are M	No A are C	All M are P	Some M are not P
All S are M	All S are C	Some S are not M	No S are M
All S are P	All S are A	Some S are not P	All S are P

Some W are H	All P are M	No G are H	No P are M
All W are K	Some M are S	All W are H	All M are S
Some K are H	Some S are P	No W are G	Some S are not P

No P are M	All P are M	All P are M
All S are M	All M are S	No S are M
Some S are not P	Some S are not P	Some S are not P

Phil. 110: Intro to Logic & Critical Thinking   Pretest 3

I. (10 points). Fill in the blank with the appropriate term or phrase.

1. According to the square of opposition, an A statement implies the

corresponding _____ proposition.

2. 'Bob is a student' is not a sentence in standard categorical form but it is best

translated as a(n) _____ categorical statement.

3. An E categorical proposition is logically equivalent to its _____ .

4. An A statement distributes its _____ term.

5. If you obvert a categorical statement with form I, the resulting statement is of
form _____ .

II. (18 points). If 'All roads lead to Rome' is true, what may we validly deduce
about the truth-values of each of the following statements? Make your verdicts
explicit.

1. No roads lead to Rome.

2. Only roads lead to Rome.

3. Some roads lead to Rome.

4. Anything that doesn't lead to Rome is no road.

III. (14 points). Make That Move. For each of the following, "make that move", by
providing the justificatory steps that lead from the first proposition to the second.
You are to use the operations on categorical sentences and the relations in the
square of opposition. (Warning: It is possible that some of the moves cannot be
made; if you find such a case, mark it as such explicitly.)

1. No C are non-S. Therefore, some S are non-C.

2. Some H are non-R. Therefore, some non-R are not non-H.

3. No S are R. Therefore, some non-R are not non-S.

IV. (20 points). Translate the following boldface claim into an appropriate categorical sentence and then use your freshly made categorical sentence to answer (b) thru (e) below. Be sure to say what your term letters stand for.

(a) **Only shallow people know themselves**

(b) form the contradictory of (a);

(c) form the contrary of (a);

(d) form the obverse of (a);

(e) form the converse of (a);

(f) Say which of (b) thru (e) is logically equivalent to (a).

V. (24 points). Test each of the following syllogisms for validity. Test the first by means of our rules, the second by Venn diagram and the third by any test you like (rules, Venn or the anti-logism test). Also, provide the mood and figure for each argument. Make your verdict about validity explicit.

1. All lions are fierce. Some lions do not drink coffee. Therefore, some creatures that drink coffee are not very fierce.

2. Some logicians are not cheaters, since all logicians are golfers and no golfers are cheaters.

3. There are mice that aren't prolific. No mice are non-rodents. Thus, there are some rodents that are non-prolific.

VI. (14 points). For each of the following enthymemes, turn it into a standard form syllogism by translating the statements into standard categorical form and then supply the missing premise or conclusion to get a valid syllogism. Also, provide the mood and figure of the resulting syllogism.

1. Some lawyers are not honest because honest people do not shade the truth.

2. Since life is short, it must be lived to the fullest.

First Logic

Final Thoughts

The heart has its reasons of which reason knows nothing.   Blaise Pascal

Man is the measure of all things: of those which are, that they are; of those which are not, that they are not.   Protagoras, 5th century B.C.E. sophist

There are two sides to every question.   Protagoras

What is Logic?

Logic is the branch of philosophy that analyzes inference

Logic is the reasoned and reasonable judgment

Logic: the principles that guide reasoning within a given field or situation

Logic: a system of reasoning

The logic of a system is the whole structure of rules that must be used for any reasoning within that system. Most of mathematics is based upon a well-understood structure of rules and is considered to be highly logical. It is always necessary to state, or otherwise have it understood, what rules are being used before any logic can be applied.

Logic is the study of the laws of thought and forms of argument

Logic is the study of reason, that is, of rational ways of drawing or establishing conclusions

The very hope of experimental philosophy, its expectation of constructing the sciences into a true philosophy of nature, is based on induction, or, if you please, the a priori presumption, that physical causation is universal; that the constitution of nature is written in its actual manifestations, and needs only to be deciphered by experimental and inductive research; that it is not a latent invisible writing, to be brought out by the magic of mental anticipation or metaphysical mediation.

What is Critical Thinking?

Critical thinking is a complex set of cognitive skills employed in problem-solving and intellectual consideration and innovation.

Critical thinking is a process that challenges an individual to use reflective, reasonable, rational thinking to gather, interpret and evaluate information in order to derive a judgment. The process involves thinking beyond a single solution for a problem and focusing on deciding what the best alternatives are.

More Thoughts on Language and Logic

From Socrates, in Plato's "Theaetetus": To use words and phrases in an easygoing manner without scrutinizing them too curiously is not, in general, a mark of ill breeding. On the contrary, there is something low brow in being too precise. But sometimes there is no help for it . . . .

From Immanuel Kant: "a canon that...serves as the principle of judging all use of the understanding as such, although only as to its rightness in respect of mere form". It is "a science a priori of the necessary laws of thinking, not, however, in respect of particular objects but all objects generatim; it is a science...of the right use of the understanding and of reason as such...i.e., according to a priori principles of how it ought to think". ...

From G.W.F. Hegel: The method of the process of Spirit's self-development "is Logic itself. For the method is nothing else than the structure of the whole in its pure and essential form." Preface, *Phenomenology of Mind*

Suggested readings

Methods of Logic, W.V. Quine
What is the Name of this Book?, Raymond Smullyan
Paradoxes from A to Z, Michael Clark
Introduction to Logic, Irving Copi and Carl Cohen
A Rulebook for Arguments, Anthony Weston
Crimes against Logic, Jamie Whyte

Logic and Philosophy on the Web

1. Funny arguments for God's existence can be found at:
   http://www.godlessgeeks.com/LINKS/GodProof.htm
   Although none of these arguments are intended as serious attempts to prove God's existence, they do have the virtue of being arguments with clear premises and conclusions.
2. Here is a website where you can find "the world's hardest logic problem":

http://philosophy.hku.hk/think/logic/hardest.php.
The site also includes material on logic in general. A useful site.

3. Here is a site devoted to jokes about philosophy and philosophers:
   http://www.workjoke.com/projoke70.htm

4. The Wikipedia entry for logic can be found at:
   http://en.wikipedia.org/wiki/Logic

5. Probably the most popular and prodigious all-purpose site for philosophy on the web is Episteme Links, at: http://www.epistemelinks.com/index.aspx

Phil. 110: Logic & Critical Thinking   Final Pretest

I. (10 points) Completion. Fill in the blank as needed.

1. All concepts are _____ to some degree or other.

2. The quality and quantity of E statements are _____
   and _____ .

3. If p and q are related such that they cannot both be true but could
   both be false then they are called _____ propositions.

4. Put a premise indicator word in the blank _____.

5. An **A** categorical statement distributes its _____ term.

II. (10 points). For exactly **two** of the following sentences, identify the propositions
it expresses and asserts (Be explicit).

1. Alan Watts is either a genius or a charlatan but he's not a Buddhist.

2. Wittgenstein is convinced that the world is all that is the case and that what is
   the case is not false.

3. Although Bob is convinced that Libby is guilty, Joe is aware Libby may be
   pardoned by Bush.

III. (16 points). For each of the following pairs of sentences determine whether they
are contraries, contradictories, or neither.

1. (a) Everybody who lives in Mankato received a "Jesus" video.
   (b) Tom lives in Mankato and he did not receive a "Jesus" video.

2. (a) No students missed the orientation session.
   (b) At least one student missed the orientation session.

3. (a) All jiggies are valuable.
   (b) Some jiggies are valuable and some aren't valuable at all.

4. (a) There's a bake sale on Friday at MSU.
   (b) There's a bake sale on Friday and Tuesday at MSU.

IV. (16 points). Identify exactly **8** fallacies from the following 10.

1. Miracles are impossible because they cannot happen.

2. Every player on the MSU hockey team is an excellent hockey player. Therefore, the MSU hockey team is going to be an excellent team this year.

3. Harvard University has an unparalleled record of scholarship. Therefore, Professor Nozicky, who is on the faculty at Harvard, must be an excellent scholar.

4. Senator X: Mr. South, did you make profitable investments with the money you obtained through your unethical use of government funds?

5. Many philosophers have tried to disprove the existence of God, but they have always failed. Since there is no disproof, I conclude that God exists.

6. **Al**: I know what caused the market crash of '52. **Bob**: What? **Al**: The sleeping problems of the director of General Motors. **Bob**: What do the sleep habits of the director of General Motors have to do with the stock market? **Al**: It crashed, didn't it?

7. Every time I wash my car, it starts to rain shortly thereafter. Therefore, my car-washing activities are causing outbursts of precipitation in the clouds.

8. I was just brought up to believe that everyone ought to have the freedom to do as they please and I have never wavered from this belief; therefore, it must be correct.

9. Capital punishment is inhumane and uncivilized, and above all, wrong. Thus, it is wrong for the government to execute wrongdoers.

10. The principle of sufficient reason is a sound reasoning principle, for it is basic to every system of reasoning in every modern culture.

V. (12 points). MAKE THAT MOVE. **Exactly two** of the following admit of makeable moves. Find those two and "make those moves".

1. Some S are not A. Thus, some non-A are S.

2. All A are B. Thus, some A are non-B.

3. No N are R. Thus, some non-R are N.

VI. (12 points). Determine the mood and figure of the following syllogisms and then test each for validity. Use a Venn diagram on 1, our rules on 2, and 3 by any of our methods that you wish (Venn, rules, or Ladd-Franklin anti-logism test).

1. All P are M
    Some S are not M
    Some S are P

2. No M are P
    All S are M
    No S are P

3. All P are M
    No S are M
    No S are P

VII. (14 points). Put the following categorical syllogism into standard form, give mood and figure, and test it for validity by Venn diagram. Make your verdict explicit and specify what your terms stand for in each case.

No one knows the trouble I've seen; it's false that no aliens know the trouble I've seen; it follows that some people are not dogs.

VIII. (10 points). For each of the following, determine whether the argument form is valid. Make your verdict explicit.

1. *p* if *q*
    not *p*
    _____
    not *q*

2. *p* if and only if *q*
    q
    _____
    p

3. If *p* then *q*
    If *q* then *r*
    _____
    If *r* then *p*

Glossary

Abstract – to abstract is to select, generalize, categorize, focus on, etc., one property to the exclusion of others; abstraction has long been a skill of mathematicians and logicians but it is also an indispensable part of language use generally

Antecedent – the first statement in an if-then statement; thus, in the statement: If p then q, the antecedent is the statement represented by 'p'

Argument – a set of three or more sentences, one of which is alleged to be supported by the others

Argument to the best explanation – a type of argument associated with the American philosopher C.S. Peirce. Peirce called these arguments abductive, contrasting them with deductive and inductive arguments. The conclusion of such an argument is an hypothesis or explanation of some event or phenomenon; these arguments, while involving a certain creative element, are judged to be better or worse by comparing them with competing arguments for different hypotheses or explanations, in part by considering the somewhat controversial notion of prior probabilities of the hypotheses in question

Assertion – offering a declarative sentence, either in print or spoken language, as true

A-statement – the universal affirmative categorical statement, All S are P

Begging the question – in ordinary parlance, it means something like, "raises the question", or "leads to the question" but in logic, it is used to refer to an argument where one of the premises is too closely related to its conclusion to make a good argument; in other words, an argument begs the question when it uses a premise that ought not to be accepted without argument by anyone who questions the truth of the argument's conclusion

Categorical logic – not surprisingly, the logic of categories or classes of things; also called Aristotelian logic, since Aristotle codified the rules and procedures of the logic of categories

Concept – in simplest terms, a concept is any general idea; typically, people speak of concepts to refer to general ideas that are rather vague or open to a variety of interpretations, thus, a concept of God, or concept of a perfect date, etc.

Concrete – typically contrasts with abstract and abstractness; most often, it is used to refer to particular objects (e.g., Fido) as opposed to concepts (e.g., dog), although some logicians do like to contrast concrete concepts to abstract concepts; thus, 'dog' is deemed to be a concrete concept while 'love' is deemed to be an abstract concept

Conditional statement – a statement of the form: If p then q

Conjunction –used in logic to designate statements of two parts that are true just when both parts are true; conjunction corresponds quite nicely to statements where 'and' (as well as its equivalents, like 'but', 'although', etc.) is the main operator of a statement

Consequence – as used in logic, it is simply another term for the result of a reasoning process; can also be used a synonym for the conclusion of an argument or for the result of an immediate inference

Consequent – the "second component" of an if-then statement; the 'q' in the statement, 'If p then q'

Contrary propositions – two propositions, p, q, are contraries just in case they cannot be simultaneously true but can both be false

Contradictory propositions – two propositions, p, q, are contradictories just in case they always have opposite truth-values; if it is the case that whenever 'p' is true, 'q' is false, and that whenever 'p' is false, 'q' is true, 'p' and 'q' are contradictory propositions; the simplest example of contradictory propositions is 'p' and 'not p'

Critical thinking – roughly speaking, critical thinking is any thinking that is devoted to the solving of some problem, the answering of a question, the clarification of ideas and, last but not least, the determination of the truth about things

Deductive soundness – a deductively valid argument, all of whose premises are true, is deductively sound

Deductive validity – any argument such that it's impossible for its premises to be true and its conclusion false is deductively valid; equivalently, any argument such that any time its premises are true, the conclusion *must* be true as well.

Definiendum and Definiens – convenient labels for the word being defined (definiendum) and the definition itself (definiens) respectively

Definition – to define a word is to provide an account of its meaning, usually by providing a brief and clear set of terms that explains what the word refers to or how to use it in various contexts

Denotation – the object that a word or name refers to or is true of; so the denotation of 'Mark Twain' is the man Mark Twain; it is basically equivalent to 'referent'

Disjunction – a term that designates an either/or statement; thus, 'p or q' is a disjunction; also known as alternation

Enthymeme – originally used to refer to an incomplete syllogism, that is, a syllogism that is missing either a premise or a conclusion; it is also used more generally for any incomplete argument, any argument that has an implicit premise or conclusion

E-statement – the universal negative categorical statement, No S are P

Fallacy – very simply, any bad argument, that is, any argument that is invalid or without force or merit can be labeled a fallacy; more commonly, fallacies are a particular sort of invalid or weak argument that is misused by the unscrupulous or committed by the careless

False/falsity – a statement is said to be false when it says of what is, that it is not, or of what is not, that it is; the opposite of true/truth, which is a property of a claim whereby it says of what is, that it is, and of what is not, that it is not

First-order logic – typically includes propositional and quantificational logic as a kind of seamless whole; the basic logic of mathematical reasoning

General terms – any term that purports to be true of more than one thing or object, for example, 'bird', 'desk', 'student', etc.; a general term can also be understood as the linguistic equivalent of a concept

Genus-differentia definitions – a definition that offers us a broad category to which the things we are trying to define belong (the genus), along with a distinguishing characteristic (the differentia) to differentiate the things we are defining from all the other members of the genus

Genus/species – relative terms that taken together express a relationship between two concepts or general terms, as follows: a concept G is genus of another concept C just in case G contains all the members of C and more besides. This relationship also means that C is a species of G.

Inconsistent propositions – statements that cannot be true at the same time or of the same world; some authors use 'inconsistent' to refer to statements that always have opposite truth-values

Inductive arguments – an argument whose premises render its conclusion likely or probable, or a good bet, but which is capable of being undermined by new information or evidence

Inductive strength – the inductive analogue of deductive validity; an inductive argument is inductively strong just in case any time its premises are true, the conclusion is likely or probably true as well

Inference – when someone claims that the truth of one statement permits us to affirm another statement, s/he is making an inference and thus performing the most basic and important of logical tasks

Intension – roughly speaking, the intension of a concept is the criteria used to determine the members of that concept, or, if you prefer, the criteria used to determine the extension of the concept

I-statement – the particular affirmative categorical statement, Some S are P

Laws of thought – traditionally, there are three laws of thought; first, the law of non-contradiction, second, the law of excluded middle, and third, the law of identity

Logic – the study of the good, the bad and the ugly in reasoning, inference and arguments, deductive and inductive

Logically equivalent statements – two statements are deemed to be logically equivalent when they are true and false in all the same cases or possible worlds

Main operator – in truth-functional logic, when a statement contains more than one truth functional operator, the main operator is the one that decides the form of the statement. Thus, a statement whose form is conjunction will have 'and' as its main operator, one whose form is disjunction will have 'or' as its main operator, and so on

Metaphor – the simplest account of a metaphor is that it is, or involves, a non-literal use of language since, literally speaking, metaphors are typically false; e.g., "Man is a wolf". Some philosophers hold that not all metaphors are false, e.g., "No man is an island". Perhaps the safest thing to say is that metaphorical language is typically problematic from a logical point of view, since it involves a kind of quirky yet instructive extension of everyday discourse, discourse that is devoted to literal use. Logically speaking, the best thing to do with a metaphor is to cash it out in more literal terms. Of course, this account leans heavily on the notion of a "literal use" of language. I shall say only that we have a fairly workable intuitive sense of this notion and that's a good thing, since cashing this notion out is not as easy as one might suppose

Necessary condition – something X is said to be a necessary condition for something Y just when Y cannot exist or occur without X; the simplest way to express this is to regard necessary conditions as the consequent of a conditional statement that has Y as the antecedent; thus, 'if Y then X' allows us to regard X as a necessary condition for Y (see also, "sufficient condition")

Negation – Negation is a truth-functional operator that governs a single statement and which results in a true statement whenever the statement it governs is false and results in a false statement whenever the statement it governs is true. Simply put, negation serves to reverse the truth-value of whatever it governs. 'Negation' can also be used to refer to the result of amending the negation operator to a sentence or statement, thus, 'not P' is the negation of 'P'

Ockham's razor – a principle of reason and science that says that theories and explanations should not multiply entities beyond necessity, or, more generally, all things being equal, simpler theories are to be preferred to more complex theories

O-statement – the particular negative categorical statement: Some S are not P

Partition – in mathematics, a partition is a division of a collection of things into mutually exclusive and jointly exhaustive subsets; in general, when classifying objects, or devising words for the purpose of classifying objects in the world, it is good practice to make use of a partition so as to avoid overlapping classes. The most common partition in logic is a two-set partition produced by the use of 'non'; thus, P and Non-P.

Propositions – the most basic use of the term is that which takes propositions to be the meanings of sentences; some logicians regard propositions as that which is communicated by a sentence; many logicians, influenced by W.V. Quine's relentless attacks on this notion of a proposition, eschew their use and prefer to speak of the use of a sentence on some particular occasion; (see also, 'statement')

Quantificational logic (also known as predicate logic) – a logic that provides symbols and rules for the use of terms like 'all' and 'at least one' (symbolized as quantifiers) as well as one-place and many-place predicates; quantificational logic was discovered/invented independently by Gottlob Frege and C.S. Peirce

Reason/reasoning – the act of using one or more claims/facts/statements to support other claims/facts/statements; 'reason' is also often used to refer to the faculty of the mind which governs and assesses our reasoning

Referent – in the philosophy of Gottlob Frege, a referent is that which is named by a proper name; more generally, it is used as a convenient label for the individual things a term names or is true of; as such, general terms have referents; indeed, they purport to have more than one referent. In contrast, proper names and definite descriptions purport to have a single referent

Semantics – the part of language study whose primary focus is on the meaning of words, that is, focused on the relation between words and what they mean, stand for, represent, symbolize, in the world.

Singular terms – any term that purports to be true of, or refer to, a single thing or object; there are two standard sorts of singular terms in language, proper names and definite descriptions

Sorites – a chain of syllogistic arguments involving three or more categorical statements; "popularized" by Lewis Carroll in his writings on logic. The term, which is Greek for 'heap', is also used to label a particular sort of logical puzzle that concerns vague terms, including terms like 'heap', 'bald'. The puzzle leans on a sort of reverse form of the mathematical principle of induction, arguing that, for example, the loss of hair will not turn a non-bald person into a bald person (or a heap into a non-heap). And yet, it is clear that at some point, removing hairs from someone's head (or stones from a heap) will yield a bald head (or a non-heap)

Statement – appreciating that different people at different times may use the same sentence to mean different things, e.g., 'I am hungry now', or 'Bob's dog is frisky', logicians feel obliged to distinguish between the sentence, understood syntactically as merely a string of symbols, and what it means on some particular occasion or use, referring to the latter as a statement; thus, a statement is a declarative sentence that states that something is true or false, as well as the content of that sentence

Sub-contraries – two propositions are sub-contraries just in case they cannot both be false at the same time but can both be true; standard example of sub-contraries are the corresponding I and O statements of categorical logic

Subset/superset – these terms mark a relation between sets of things as follows; a set A, all of whose members are included in another set B, is said to be a subset of B; if B also contains more than just the members of A, B is called a superset of A. All sets are deemed to be subsets of themselves but no set can be a superset of itself

Sufficient condition – X is a sufficient condition for Y if the presence of X is incompatible with the non-presence of Y. More simply, perhaps, if any time X occurs, Y occurs, X is a sufficient condition for Y

Syllogism – classically, it means a rather specific form of argument first set out in Aristotle's treatises on logic collectively referred to as the *Organon* (literally, tool or instrument); a syllogism consists of two categorical propositions as premises and a categorical proposition as a conclusion, and which contains exactly three terms. It is common today to call almost any two premise/one conclusion argument a syllogism

Syntax – the part of language study that concerns the more formal aspects of the symbols and signs of language, aspects like the shape, position, size, number of symbols in contrast to what the symbols mean or refer to

Tautology – from the Greek for "same word", it refers to statements like, 'A rose is a rose', or 'I want what I want'; it is also used to identify statements of truth-functional logic that are true on any interpretations of their component statements, thus, 'If p then p', and 'p or not p' are tautologies

True/truth – a statement is true when it says of what is that it is or of what is not that it is not; – it is the opposite of false/falsity, which is a property of a claim whereby it says of what is, that it is not, or of what is not, that it is

Truth-functional logic – the logic of truth functions, including especially the logic of 'and', 'or', 'if-then', 'not' and 'if and only if'. Although the origins of truth-functional logic can be traced back to the Stoics (roughly 350 BCE), truth-functional logic became prominent in the early 20th century with the work of Gottlob Frege and Russell and Whitehead.

Truth-tables – a table that graphically displays the truth-values of a truth-functional statement, given the truth-values of its component statements; truth-tables can also be seen as a way of setting out the "meaning" of the truth-functional connective to which it corresponds be